3 1705 00319 2314

TRADITIONAL IRiSH COOKERY

CARMEL KAVENAGH

D1491205

foulsham
LONDON • NEW YORK • TORONTO • SYDNEY

foulsham

The Publishing House, Bennetts Close, Cippenham,
Berkshire, SL1 5AP, England

ISBN 0-572-02684-6

Copyright © 2001 W. Foulsham & Co. Ltd

Main cover photograph © The Image Bank
Small cover photographs (left and right) © James Jackson
Small cover photograph (centre) © The Image Bank

All rights reserved.

The Copyright Act prohibits (subject to certain
very limited exceptions) the making of copies of
any copyright work or of a substantial part of such
a work, including the making of copies by
photocopying or similar process. Written
permission to make a copy or copies must
therefore normally be obtained from the publisher
in advance. It is advisable also to consult the
publisher if in any doubt as to the legality of any
copying which is to be undertaken.

Printed in Great Britain by The Bath Press, Bath

Contents

Introduction

When we think about Irish cookery, we usually think about good, wholesome fare made from fresh, local ingredients. It is certainly true that the Irish, who are still predominantly a rural community, have a robust style of cooking that takes advantage of the range of ingredients available to them, from quality beef and dairy products from the pastures, through fish from the surrounding seas and productive rivers, to vegetables and fruits from the fields and orchards.

Ireland's staple food for many generations was the potato, and even nowadays this humble vegetable features heavily on the menu, but in many different guises. Many other vegetables that thrive in the maritime climate – such as parsnips, cabbage, leeks and turnips – are also cooked in a variety of ways and served both as accompaniments and as ingredients in stews and casseroles.

With the relatively generous rainfall encouraging lush, lowland pastures that are ideal for grazing, high-quality beef is farmed both for the home and export markets, and Ireland has an enviable reputation as a supplier of excellent beef. Many cattle are also raised in dairy farms, producing milk, butter and cream.

The higher pastures are suitable for raising sheep, and today's farms produce lamb, rather than the mutton and kid that used to form the basis of the famous Irish stew. Pigs are also raised, predominantly for bacon and hams, while game and venison remain popular.

As an island nation, many of the first communities grew up around the coast, so fish was a staple part of the diet, and all kinds of fish still form an important element of today's menus. Salmon and perch from the rivers and lakes, and lobster, Dublin Bay prawns (shrimp), skate, plaice and mackerel from the seas are just a few of the delights available.

With plenty of home-grown cereals, including oats and barley, baking remains an important part of domestic life, so home-baked breads and cakes are popular, sometimes flavoured with a dram of Irish whiskey or stout. Whiskey and stout also find their way into casseroles and sauces, giving a rich flavour as well as tenderising the slow-cooked meat. Orchard fruits, such as apples, feature heavily in both cakes and breads, and are also cooked with vegetables to be served with strongly flavoured meats such as pork and bacon.

With such a range of wholesome ingredients, it is no wonder that Ireland can offer us a varied, interesting and healthy collection of recipes. I hope you enjoy sharing this selection.

Notes on the Recipes

- Do not mix metric, imperial and American measures. Follow one set only.
- American terms are given in brackets.
- All spoon measurements are level: 1 tsp = 5 ml;
  1 tbsp = 15 ml.
- Eggs are medium unless otherwise stated. If you use a different size, adjust the amount of liquid added to obtain the right consistency.
- Always wash, peel, core and seed, if necessary, fresh foods before use. Ensure that all produce is as fresh as possible and in good condition.
- Seasoning and the use of strongly flavoured ingredients, such as onions and garlic, are very much a matter of personal taste. Taste the food as you cook and adjust seasoning to suit your own taste.
- Always use fresh herbs unless dried are specifically called for. If you do use dried herbs, use half the quantity stated. Chopped frozen varieties are much better than dried. There is no substitute for fresh parsley and coriander (cilantro).
- A fresh bouquet garni is traditionally made up of sprigs of thyme, parsley and bay leaf tied together with string or wrapped in muslin (cheesecloth), and is used in slow-cooked dishes. Sachets of dried bouquet garni are readily available.
- Can and packet sizes are approximate and will depend on the particular brand.
- Use whichever kitchen gadgets you like to speed up preparation and cooking: mixers for whisking, food processors for grating, slicing, mixing or kneading and blenders for liquidising.
- Always preheat the oven (unless using a fan-assisted oven) and cook on the centre shelf unless otherwise specified. All ovens vary, so cooking times have to be approximate.

Soups

Usually based on vegetables and thickened with potatoes, soups make a nourishing start to a meal, or a meal in themselves if teamed with crusty bread. Soda Bread (page 106) makes a great accompaniment, and if you have some stale bread, you can place a slice in the bottom of the soup bowl and pour over the hot soup to add flavour and texture to the meal. Vary the ingredients depending on the season and on what you have available, and add your favourite fresh herbs to lift the taste.

Bacon and Cabbage Broth

Serves 4

	METRIC	IMPERIAL	AMERICAN
Lard (shortening) or bacon fat	15 ml	1 tbsp	1 tbsp
Streaky bacon rashers (slices), rinded and chopped	225 g	8 oz	8 oz
Onion, chopped	1	1	1
Carrot, chopped	1	1	1
Celery stick, chopped	1	1	1
Small turnip, chopped	1	1	1
White cabbage, chopped	350 g	12 oz	12 oz
Vegetable or chicken stock or water	1.2 litres	2 pts	5 cups
Salt and freshly ground black pepper			
Slices of toast	4	4	4

1 Melt the lard or bacon fat in a large saucepan and fry (sauté) the bacon, onion, carrot, celery and turnip until softened but not browned.

2 Stir in the cabbage until all the ingredients are well mixed and coated in the fat.

3 Add the stock or water and season with salt and pepper. Bring to the boil, then reduce the heat and simmer gently for about 45 minutes until the vegetables are tender. Check and adjust the seasoning to taste.

4 Place a slice of toast in the base of four warmed soup bowls and spoon over the soup to serve.

⊕ **Preparation and cooking time:** 1 hour

Leek Soup

SERVES 4

	METRIC	IMPERIAL	AMERICAN
Milk	600 ml	1 pt	2½ cups
Butter or margarine	25 g	1 oz	2 tbsp
Medium oatmeal	30 ml	2 tbsp	2 tbsp
Large leeks, chopped	3	3	3
Salt and freshly ground black pepper			
Chopped fresh parsley	15 ml	1 tbsp	1 tbsp
Wholemeal Soda Bread (page 107), to serve			

1 Bring the milk and butter or margarine to the boil in a large saucepan.

2 Stir in the oatmeal and simmer, stirring, for 1 minute.

3 Add the leeks and season with salt and pepper. Return to the boil, reduce the heat, cover and simmer gently for about 30 minutes until the leeks are tender.

4 Stir in the parsley and check and adjust the seasoning to taste. Simmer for 5 minutes, then serve with soda bread.

🕐 **Preparation and cooking time:** 40 minutes

Mutton Broth

Since mutton is no longer readily available, you can make this tasty soup with lamb. It is best made a day in advance.

SERVES 4

	METRIC	IMPERIAL	AMERICAN
Neck of mutton or lamb	900 g	2 lb	2 lb
Water	1.5 litres	2½ cups	6 cups
Pearl barley	30 ml	2 tbsp	2 tbsp
Onion, chopped	1	1	1
Turnip, chopped	1	1	1
Carrots, chopped	2	2	2
Small white cabbage, shredded	½	½	½
Salt and freshly ground black pepper			

1 Place the mutton or lamb and water in a large saucepan, bring to the boil, then skim the surface. Add the pearl barley, reduce the heat, cover and simmer gently for about 1½ hours until the meat is very tender.

2 Skim again, if necessary. Add the vegetables, return to the boil, reduce the heat, cover and simmer gently for a further 1 hour.

3 Remove the meat from the pan, discard the bones and any gristle, chop the meat and return it to the pan. Leave to cool and chill, overnight if possible.

4 Remove and discard the fat that will have solidified on the surface, then reheat the broth. Check and adjust the seasoning before serving in warmed bowls.

⏱ **Preparation and cooking time:** 2¾ hours plus chilling

Nettle Soup

Collect fresh nettle tops for this traditional soup from open countryside away from roads and animals. To measure the quantity, simply press them gently into a basin. You can also make the recipe with sorrel.

SERVES 4

	METRIC	IMPERIAL	AMERICAN
Butter or margarine	25 g	1 oz	2 tbsp
Medium oatmeal	50 g	2 oz	½ cup
Vegetable stock	1.2 litres	2 pts	5 cups
Nettle tops, finely chopped	1.2 litres	2 pts	5 cups
Salt and freshly ground black pepper			

1 Melt the butter or margarine in a large saucepan and fry (sauté) the oatmeal until golden, stirring continuously.

2 Add the stock and bring to the boil, then add the nettles and season with salt and pepper. Reduce the heat and simmer for about 40 minutes until tender and well blended.

3 Purée in a food processor or blender, then return to the pan to reheat before serving.

🕐 **Preparation and cooking time:** 50 minutes

Parsnip and Apple Soup

SERVES 4

	METRIC	IMPERIAL	AMERICAN
Butter or margarine	*15 g*	*½ oz*	*1 tbsp*
Onion, chopped	*1*	*1*	*1*
Parsnips, thinly sliced	*450 g*	*1 lb*	*1 lb*
Garlic clove, crushed	*1*	*1*	*1*
Cooking (tart) apples, peeled, cored and sliced	*450 g*	*1 lb*	*1 lb*
Curry powder	*10 ml*	*2 tsp*	*2 tsp*
Ground cumin	*5 ml*	*1 tsp*	*1 tsp*
Ground coriander (cilantro)	*5 ml*	*1 tsp*	*1 tsp*
Chicken or vegetable stock	*1.2 litres*	*2 pts*	*5 cups*
Salt and freshly ground black pepper			
Single (light) cream	*150 ml*	*¼ pt*	*⅔ cup*
Snipped fresh chives	*15 ml*	*1 tbsp*	*1 tbsp*

1 Melt the butter or margarine in a large saucepan and fry (sauté) the onion until just beginning to soften. Add the parsnips, garlic and apples and cook until softened but not browned.

2 Stir in the spices and cook for 2 minutes, stirring. Add the stock and bring to the boil, stirring continuously. Season with salt and pepper, then reduce the heat, cover and simmer gently for about 30 minutes until the parsnips are tender.

3 Purée in a food processor or blender or rub through a sieve (strainer), then return to the pan and stir in the cream. Thin down with a little more stock or water, if preferred. Taste and adjust the seasoning and reheat gently, without allowing the soup to boil.

4 Serve sprinkled with chives.

☉ **Preparation and cooking time:** 45 minutes

Pea and Ham Soup

SERVES 4

	METRIC	IMPERIAL	AMERICAN
Butter or margarine	25 g	1 oz	2 tbsp
Onion, chopped	1	1	1
Vegetable stock	600 ml	1 pt	2½ cups
Milk	120 ml	4 fl oz	½ cup
Cooked potatoes, diced	225 g	8 oz	8 oz
Frozen peas	175 g	6 oz	6 oz
Cooked ham, diced	100 g	4 oz	1 cup
Chopped fresh parsley	15 ml	1 tbsp	1 tbsp
Salt and freshly ground black pepper			
Single (light) cream (optional)	15 ml	1 tbsp	1 tbsp
Soda Bread (page 106), to serve			

1 Melt half the butter or margarine in a large saucepan and fry (sauté) the onion until softened but not browned.

2 Add the stock and milk and bring to the boil.

3 Add the potatoes and peas, reduce the heat and simmer for about 15 minutes until the peas are tender and the potatoes are beginning to fall apart.

4 Purée in a food processor or blender, then return to the pan and stir in the ham and parsley. Season with salt and pepper and stir in the cream, if liked. Heat through before serving with soda bread.

⏱ **Preparation and cooking time:** 30 minutes

Potato and Fresh Herb Soup

SERVES 4

	METRIC	IMPERIAL	AMERICAN
Butter or margarine	25 g	1 oz	2 tbsp
Onions, chopped	450 g	1 lb	1 lb
Lean bacon rashers (slices), rinded and chopped	2	2	2
Potatoes, chopped	450 g	1 lb	1 lb
Carrot, chopped	1	1	1
Vegetable stock	900 ml	1½ pts	3¾ cups
Milk	300 ml	½ pt	1¼ cups
Salt and freshly ground black pepper			
Single (light) cream	150 ml	¼ pt	⅔ cup
Chopped fresh parsley	30 ml	2 tbsp	2 tbsp
Snipped fresh chives	15 ml	1 tbsp	1 tbsp

1 Melt the butter or margarine in a large saucepan and fry (sauté) the onions and bacon for about 5 minutes until softened but not browned.

2 Add the potatoes and carrot and fry for 10 minutes, stirring occasionally.

3 Add the stock and milk, and season with salt and pepper. Bring to the boil, reduce the heat, cover and simmer for about 30 minutes until the vegetables are tender.

4 Purée in a food processor or blender, then return the soup to the pan, check and adjust the seasoning and stir in the cream and parsley. Reheat gently and serve sprinkled with the chives.

⏲ **Preparation and cooking time:** 50 minutes

Turnip Soup

SERVES 4

	METRIC	IMPERIAL	AMERICAN
Lard (shortening) or vegetable fat	25 g	1 oz	2 tbsp
Streaky bacon rashers (slices), rinded and chopped	100 g	4 oz	4 oz
Onion, chopped	1	1	1
Potato, peeled and chopped	1	1	1
Turnips, chopped	450 g	1 lb	1 lb
Vegetable or chicken stock	1.2 litres	2 pts	5 cups
Salt and freshly ground black pepper			
Soda Bread (page 106), to serve			

1 Melt the lard or vegetable fat and fry (sauté) the bacon and onion until softened but not browned.

2 Add the potato and turnips and fry, stirring, until all the ingredients are browned and well mixed. Add the stock and season with salt and pepper. Bring to the boil, then reduce the heat, cover and simmer gently for about 20 minutes until all the vegetables are cooked.

3 Adjust the seasoning to taste and serve with soda bread.

⏱ **Preparation and cooking time:** 35 minutes

Vegetable Skink

Skink is a Gaelic term for broth, and this particular recipe makes a flavoursome broth with mixed vegetables.

SERVES 4

	METRIC	IMPERIAL	AMERICAN
Celery sticks, chopped	3	3	3
Cos (romaine) lettuce leaves, chopped	6	6	6
Frozen peas	100 g	4 oz	4 oz
Spring onions (scallions), chopped	4	4	4
Vegetable stock	750 ml	1¼ pts	3 cups
Sprigs of parsley	3	3	3
Sprig of thyme	1	1	1
A few chive stalks			
Bay leaf	1	1	1
Double (heavy) cream	75 ml	5 tbsp	5 tbsp
Egg yolk	1	1	1
Salt and freshly ground black pepper			
Chopped fresh parsley	15 ml	1 tbsp	1 tbsp

1 Place the vegetables and stock in a large saucepan. Tie the parsley, thyme, chives and bay leaf together, then add to the pan. Bring to the boil, reduce the heat, then cover and simmer for 30 minutes until the vegetables are tender. Discard the herbs.

2 Blend together the cream and egg yolk, stir it into the soup and heat through gently without boiling.

3 Season to taste with salt and pepper and serve sprinkled with the chopped parsley.

⏲ **Preparation and cooking time:** 45 minutes

Lamb and Beef

Many of the recipes given for lamb would traditionally have been made with mutton, which has a stronger flavour and requires a slightly longer cooking time. However, since this is no longer readily available, you can use lamb instead.

In the past, when everything was used and nothing wasted, a favourite country recipe was lambs' tongues, which were soaked for two days in salted water with saltpetre – very hard to obtain now as it is an ingredient of gunpowder! – then boiled with herbs and served hot with onion sauce. The tongues are now a fairly rare item at the butcher, but you can still find them at specialist outlets if you want to try this very traditional recipe. Another Irish speciality is Drisheen, a white blood pudding made with sheep's blood, which is boiled and served with a parsley sauce seasoned with mace.

Irish Stew

Every Irish farmer's wife has her own recipe for this rich stew, made with lamb and vegetables, and varies it with the ingredients available according to the season.

SERVES 4

	METRIC	IMPERIAL	AMERICAN
Oil	15 ml	1 tbsp	1 tbsp
Stewing lamb, cubed	900 g	2 lb	2 lb
Onions, sliced	2	2	2
Carrots, thickly sliced	3	3	3
Celery sticks, chopped	2	2	2
Leek, sliced	1	1	1
Potatoes, thickly sliced	450 g	1 lb	1 lb
Water	600 ml	1 pt	2½ cups
Chopped fresh parsley	30 ml	2 tbsp	2 tbsp
Chopped fresh thyme	5 ml	1 tsp	1 tsp
Bay leaf	1	1	1
Salt and freshly ground black pepper			
A sprig of parsley, to garnish			

1 Heat the oil in a heavy-based saucepan and fry (sauté) the lamb until sealed on all sides. Add the onions, carrots, celery and leek and fry for 2 minutes. Add the potatoes.

2 Pour in just enough water to cover the ingredients, add the herbs and season with salt and pepper.

3 Bring to the boil, then reduce the heat, cover and simmer very gently for about 1¾ hours until all the ingredients are tender and the sauce is thick. Taste and adjust the seasoning if necessary.

4 Serve garnished with parsley.

☉ **Preparation and cooking time:** 2 hours

Lamb Slices with Minted Peas and Cream

SERVES 4

	METRIC	IMPERIAL	AMERICAN
Plain (all-purpose) flour	15 ml	1 tbsp	1 tbsp
Salt and freshly ground black pepper			
Lamb steaks, sliced	450 g	1 lb	1 lb
Lard (shortening)	15 g	½ oz	1 tbsp
Vegetable stock	150 ml	¼ pt	⅔ cup
Shelled fresh or frozen peas	450 g	1 lb	1 lb
A few sprigs of mint			
Single (light) cream	150 ml	¼ pt	⅔ cup
Chopped fresh mint	15 ml	1 tbsp	1 tbsp
Boiled new potatoes, to serve			

1 Season the flour with salt and pepper and toss the lamb in the flour, shaking off any excess.

2 Heat the lard in a heavy-based frying pan (skillet) and fry (sauté) the lamb slices until sealed on all sides. Stir in the stock and bring to the boil, stirring continuously, then reduce the heat to minimum, cover and simmer gently for about 20 minutes until the lamb is tender.

3 Meanwhile, bring a large pan of salted water to the boil, add the peas and mint sprigs, then reduce the heat and simmer for about 15 minutes until tender. If you are using frozen peas, you will only need to cook them for about 5 minutes.

4 Drain well, discarding the mint, then return to the pan and stir in the cream. Warm through gently, stir in the chopped mint and season with salt and pepper.

5 Serve the lamb and minted peas with new potatoes.

☉ **Preparation and cooking time:** 35 minutes

Lamb and Vegetable Pie

SERVES 4

	METRIC	IMPERIAL	AMERICAN
Lard (shortening) or vegetable fat	25 g	1 oz	2 tbsp
Onion, chopped	1	1	1
Carrots, chopped	2	2	2
Celery stick, chopped	1	1	1
Lean stewing lamb, diced	450 g	1 lb	1 lb
Rich stock or gravy	600 ml	1 pt	2½ cups
Salt and freshly ground black pepper			
Cornflour (cornstarch)	15 ml	1 tbsp	1 tbsp
Potatoes, peeled and quartered	900 g	2 lb	2 lb
Butter or margarine	50 g	2 oz	¼ cup
Seasonal vegetables, to serve			

1 Heat the lard or vegetable fat in a large saucepan and fry (sauté) the onion, carrots and celery until softened but not browned. Add the lamb and fry until sealed on all sides.

2 Pour in the stock or gravy and season with salt and pepper. Bring to the boil, then reduce the heat, cover and simmer gently for about 45 minutes until the meat is very tender.

3 If the gravy is not thick enough, mix the cornflour to a paste with a little water, then blend into the gravy and simmer, stirring, until thickened. Spoon into a casserole dish (Dutch oven).

4 Meanwhile, cook the potatoes in boiling salted water until tender, then drain and mash with most of the butter or margarine. Spoon over the lamb and dot with the remaining butter or margarine.

5 Bake in a preheated oven at 190°C/375°F/gas mark 5 for about 30 minutes until heated through and golden brown on top. Serve with seasonal vegetables.

🕐 **Preparation and cooking time:** 1½ hours

Lamb Chops with Broad Beans

SERVES 4

	METRIC	IMPERIAL	AMERICAN
Broad (fava) beans	225 g	8 oz	8 oz
Butter or margarine	50 g	2 oz	¼ cup
Shallots, chopped	2	2	2
Lamb chump chops	4	4	4
Salt and freshly ground black pepper			
Chopped fresh rosemary	2.5 ml	½ tsp	½ tsp
Tomatoes, skinned and sliced	4	4	4
Vegetable stock	250 ml	8 fl oz	1 cup
Mashed potatoes, to serve			

1 Bring a large pan of water to the boil, add the broad beans, then reduce the heat and simmer for about 15 minutes until tender. The cooking time will vary depending on the freshness of the beans. Drain and arrange half in the base of a large casserole dish (Dutch oven).

2 Melt half the butter or margarine and fry (sauté) the shallots until transparent, then add the chops and fry until browned on both sides. Place the shallots and chops on top of the beans. Season with salt and pepper and sprinkle with rosemary.

3 Arrange the tomatoes over the top and finish with the remaining beans. Pour over the stock and cover tightly.

4 Bake in a preheated oven at 180°C/350°F/gas mark 4 for about 1½ hours until the meat is tender, checking and adding a little more stock or water if necessary during cooking.

5 Serve with mashed potatoes.

⏲ **Preparation and cooking time:** 2 hours

Apple-stuffed Lamb in Cider

SERVES 4

	METRIC	IMPERIAL	AMERICAN
Cooking (tart) apples, peeled, cored and chopped	2	2	2
Juice of 1 lemon			
Caster (superfine) sugar	15 ml	1 tbsp	1 tbsp
Ground ginger	5 ml	1 tsp	1 tsp
Boned loin of lamb	900 g	2 lb	2 lb
Garlic cloves, cut into slivers	2	2	2
Salt and freshly ground black pepper			
Dry cider	250 ml	8 fl oz	1 cup
Mashed potatoes and a green vegetable, to serve			

1 Place the apples, lemon juice, sugar and ginger in a saucepan and simmer gently for about 10 minutes until soft. Remove from the heat and leave to cool.

2 Remove the skin from the lamb and score the fat. Place the meat, fat-side down, on a work surface, open out and spoon the apple mixture along the centre. Roll up and tie with cooks' string.

3 Make cuts all over the outside of the meat with the point of a sharp knife, then press the slivers of garlic into the meat. Season all over with salt and pepper and place in a roasting tin (pan).

4 Warm the cider in a small saucepan, then pour it over the lamb.

5 Roast in a preheated oven at 200°C/400°F/gas mark 6 for 30 minutes, then reduce the oven temperature to 180°C/350°F/gas mark 4 and cook for a further 40 minutes until tender, basting frequently.

6 Transfer the lamb to a warmed serving dish, cover with foil and keep warm.

7 Remove any excess fat from the roasting tin, then boil the juices for 1–2 minutes until reduced slightly.

8 Slice the lamb, pour over the cooking juices and serve with mashed potatoes and a green vegetable.

⏱ **Preparation and cooking time:** 1¾ hours

Roast Lamb with Mustard

SERVES 4

	METRIC	IMPERIAL	AMERICAN
Plain (all-purpose) flour	15 ml	1 tbsp	1 tbsp
Mustard powder	15 ml	1 tbsp	1 tbsp
Salt and freshly ground black pepper			
Leg or shoulder of lamb	900 g	2 lb	2 lb
Roast potatoes and a selection of vegetables, to serve			

1 Mix together the flour and mustard and season with salt and pepper. Rub over the surface of the lamb.

2 Roast in a preheated oven at 220°C/425°F/gas mark 7 for 15 minutes, then reduce the oven temperature to 180°C/350°F/gas mark 4 and continue to cook for a further 1 hour or until the lamb is cooked to your liking.

3 Remove from the oven, cover with foil and leave to rest for 15 minutes before carving and serving with roast potatoes and vegetables.

⏱ **Preparation and cooking time:** 1½ hours

Liver and Bacon with Onion Gravy

SERVES 4

	METRIC	IMPERIAL	AMERICAN
Lard (shortening) or vegetable fat	15 g	½ oz	1 tbsp
Onion, sliced	1	1	1
Plain (all-purpose) flour	15 ml	1 tbsp	1 tbsp
Salt and freshly ground black pepper			
Lambs' liver, sliced	450 g	1 lb	1 lb
Chicken or vegetable stock	450 ml	¾ pt	2 cups
Back bacon rashers (slices), rinded	450 g	1 lb	1 lb
Mashed potatoes and carrots, to serve			

1 Heat the lard or vegetable fat in a large frying pan (skillet) and fry (sauté) the onion until just beginning to turn golden.

2 Season the flour with salt and pepper and toss the liver slices in the flour, shaking off any excess. Add to the pan and fry until sealed on all sides.

3 Add the stock and bring to the boil, stirring well. Reduce the heat and leave to simmer gently for about 15 minutes until the liver is just tender.

4 Meanwhile, grill (broil) the bacon rashers until crisp.

5 Spoon the liver and the onion gravy into a warmed, deep serving dish and arrange the bacon on a separate plate. Serve with mashed potatoes and carrots.

⏱ **Preparation and cooking time:** 30 minutes

Roast Beef with Whiskey

SERVES 4-6

	METRIC	IMPERIAL	AMERICAN
Boned rib of beef	1.5 kg	3 lb	3 lb
Salt and freshly ground black pepper			
Irish whiskey	60 ml	4 tbsp	4 tbsp
Red wine	300 ml	½ pt	1¼ cups
Butter or margarine	25 g	1 oz	2 tbsp
Plain (all-purpose) flour	50 g	2 oz	½ cup
Roast potatoes and seasonal vegetables, to serve			

1 Season the meat with salt and pepper, place in a roasting tin (pan) and roast in a preheated oven at 180°C/350°F/gas mark 4 for 1 hour.

2 Pour the whiskey and wine over the meat and return to the oven for a further 1 hour or until cooked to your liking, basting occasionally.

3 Transfer the meat to a serving plate, cover with foil and keep it warm.

4 Skim off any excess fat from the roasting tin and make up the remaining juices to about 450 ml/¾ pt/2 cups with water.

5 Blend together the butter or margarine and flour to make a roux, then whisk it, a little at a time, into the juices and heat gently until the gravy thickens. Continue to cook for 3 minutes, stirring continuously.

6 Slice the meat and serve with roast potatoes and seasonal vegetables, with the gravy served separately.

⏱ **Preparation and cooking time:** 2¼ hours

Beef with Guinness

Cooking meat in alcohol tenderises tough cuts and Guinness, the traditional Irish drink, makes the dish rich and flavoursome.

SERVES 4

	METRIC	IMPERIAL	AMERICAN
Plain (all-purpose) flour	30 ml	2 tbsp	2 tbsp
Salt and freshly ground black pepper			
Shin of beef, cut into chunks	900 g	2 lb	2 lb
Beef dripping or lard (shortening)	30 ml	2 tbsp	2 tbsp
Onions, sliced	2	2	2
Carrots, sliced	4	4	4
Guinness or Irish stout	150 ml	¼ pt	⅔ cup
Water	150 ml	¼ pt	⅔ cup
Chopped fresh parsley	15 ml	1 tbsp	1 tbsp
Boiled potatoes, to serve			

1 Season the flour with salt and pepper. Toss the beef in the seasoned flour, shaking off any excess.

2 Heat the dripping or lard in a large, heavy-based saucepan and fry (sauté) the beef until lightly browned on all sides. Remove from the pan.

3 Add the onions to the pan and fry until softened but not browned. Add the beef and carrots, stir well, then pour over the Guinness or stout and water. Bring to the boil, then reduce the heat, cover and simmer gently for 1½–2 hours until the meat is tender and the sauce is thick, adding a little more liquid during cooking if necessary.

4 Sprinkle with parsley and serve with boiled potatoes.

🕐 **Preparation and cooking time:** 1¾–2¼ hours

Spiced Beef

A traditional Christmas dish, this takes some time to make but is delicious. The spice mixture used to include 10 ml/2 tsp saltpetre to give the meat a pink colour, but this is now almost impossible to obtain.

SERVES 12

	METRIC	IMPERIAL	AMERICAN
Salt	100 g	4 oz	½ cup
Ground cloves	10 ml	2 tsp	2 tsp
Freshly ground black pepper	10 ml	2 tsp	2 tsp
Ground allspice	10 ml	2 tsp	2 tsp
Ground cinnamon	10 ml	2 tsp	2 tsp
Ground mace	10 ml	2 tsp	2 tsp
Black treacle (molasses)	30 ml	2 tbsp	2 tbsp
Soft brown sugar	30 ml	2 tbsp	2 tbsp
Topside or silverside of beef	2.75 kg	6 lb	6 lb
Guinness or Irish stout	300 ml	½ pt	⅔ cup

1 Mix together the salt, spices, treacle and sugar. Place the beef in a small, deep bowl and add the spice mixture, rubbing it into the meat. Cover and place in the fridge for 1 week, rubbing the mixture into the meat once or twice a day.

2 Tie the meat into a neat shape and place it in a heavy-based saucepan. Pour over the Guinness or stout, then add enough water to cover the meat. Bring to the boil, then reduce the heat, cover and simmer gently for 5 hours until the meat is tender.

3 Leave the meat to cool in the liquid, then remove and leave to drain.

4 Serve thinly sliced.

🕐 **Preparation and cooking time:** 5 hours plus soaking

Beef Stew and Parsley Dumplings

SERVES 4

	METRIC	IMPERIAL	AMERICAN
Oil	30 ml	2 tbsp	2 tbsp
Onions, chopped	2	2	2
Garlic clove, chopped	1	1	1
Bacon rashers (slices), rinded and chopped	100 g	4 oz	4 oz
Carrot, sliced	1	1	1
Mushrooms, sliced	100 g	4 oz	4 oz
Braising steak, cubed	450 g	1 lb	1 lb
Plain (all-purpose) flour	15 ml	1 tbsp	1 tbsp
Beef or chicken stock	600 ml	1 pt	2½ cups
Tomatoes, skinned and chopped	4	4	4
Chopped fresh parsley	15 ml	1 tbsp	1 tbsp
Salt and freshly ground black pepper			
For the dumplings:			
Self-raising (self-rising) flour	100 g	4 oz	1 cup
Shredded (chopped) suet	50 g	2 oz	½ cup
Chopped fresh parsley	15 ml	1 tbsp	1 tbsp
Salt and freshly ground black pepper			
Water	30 ml	2 tbsp	2 tbsp

1 Heat the oil in a large saucepan and fry (sauté) the onions, garlic, bacon and carrot until the onion is softened but not browned. Add the mushrooms and fry until moist.

2 Stir in the meat and fry until browned, then sprinkle with flour and cook, stirring, for 1 minute. Stir in the stock, then add the tomatoes and parsley and season to taste with salt and pepper. Bring to the boil, then reduce the heat, partially cover and simmer for about 1 hour until the meat is tender.

3 Meanwhile, make the dumplings. Mix together the flour, suet and parsley and season with salt and pepper. Gradually stir in enough of the water to make a stiff dough. Shape into eight balls, using floured hands.

4 Add the dumplings to the stew, cover and continue to cook for about 25 minutes until cooked through.

⏲ **Preparation and cooking time:** 1¾ hours

Minced Beef and Mushroom Pie

SERVES 4

	METRIC	IMPERIAL	AMERICAN
Beef dripping or lard (shortening)	15 g	½ oz	1 tbsp
Streaky bacon rashers (slices), rinded and chopped	3	3	3
Large onions, finely chopped	2	2	2
Minced (ground) beef	450 g	1 lb	1 lb
Mushrooms, sliced	225 g	8 oz	8 oz
Plain (all-purpose) flour	15 ml	1 tbsp	1 tbsp
Tomato purée (paste)	15 ml	1 tbsp	1 tbsp
Beef stock	250 ml	8 fl oz	1 cup
Chopped fresh parsley	5 ml	1 tsp	1 tsp
Chopped fresh thyme	5 ml	1 tsp	1 tsp
Chopped fresh sage	5 ml	1 tsp	1 tsp
Salt and freshly ground black pepper			
Frozen puff pastry (paste), thawed	350 g	12 oz	12 oz
A little milk, for glazing			
Seasonal vegetables, to serve			

1 Melt the dripping or lard in a heavy-based frying pan (skillet) and fry (sauté) the bacon and onions until softened but not browned.

2 Stir in the beef and cook until browned and all the grains are separate. Add the mushrooms and fry for 1 minute. Sprinkle over the flour and stir into the meat, then stir in the tomato purée.

3 Add the stock and herbs and season with salt and pepper. Bring to the boil, then reduce the heat, cover and simmer for about 20 minutes until the meat is cooked and the sauce is thick. Remove the lid towards the end of cooking if the sauce is not thick enough, to allow the liquid to reduce.

4 Place a baking (cookie) sheet in the oven and heat to 200°C/400°F/gas mark 6.

5 Roll out the pastry on a lightly floured surface and use half to line a greased 23 cm/9 in pie dish. Spoon in the meat mixture. Cut the remaining pastry to make a lid, moisten the edges and seal to the base. Decorate with the trimmings and brush with beaten egg.

6 Place the dish on the hot baking sheet and bake in the preheated oven for 25 minutes until golden brown.

7 Serve with fresh vegetables.

⏲ **Preparation and cooking time:** 1 hour

Porter Beef

SERVES 4

	METRIC	IMPERIAL	AMERICAN
Plain (all-purpose) flour	30 ml	2 tbsp	2 tbsp
Grated nutmeg	1.5 ml	¼ tsp	¼ tsp
Salt and freshly ground black pepper			
Shin of beef, cut into chunks	900 g	2 lb	2 lb
Beef dripping or lard (shortening)	30 ml	2 tbsp	2 tbsp
Onions, chopped	3	3	3
Mushrooms, sliced	100 g	4 oz	4 oz
Soft brown sugar	5 ml	1 tsp	1 tsp
Porter or Irish stout	300 ml	½ pt	1⅓ cups
Water	150 ml	¼ pt	⅔ cup
Boiled potatoes, to serve			

1 Season the flour with nutmeg, salt and pepper. Toss the beef in the seasoned flour, shaking off any excess.

2 Heat the dripping or lard in a large, heavy-based saucepan and fry (sauté) the beef until lightly browned on all sides. Remove from the pan.

3 Add the onions to the pan and fry until softened but not browned. Add the mushrooms and stir well, then stir in the beef and sugar.

4 Pour over the porter or stout and water, bring to the boil, then reduce the heat, cover and simmer gently for 1½–2 hours until the meat is tender and the sauce is thick, adding a little more liquid during cooking if necessary. Serve with boiled potatoes.

⏱ **Preparation and cooking time:** 1¾–2¼ hours

Pork, Bacon and Ham

There are many interesting Irish pork, bacon and ham recipes, and most of them taste particularly good in apple-based vegetable recipes or served with apple sauce or Apple Jelly (page 43). Traditionally, of course, the recipes would use local ingredients, such as hams smoked over juniper branches to give them a subtle but distinctive flavour.

Pork products always formed the basis of the traditional Irish farmhouse breakfast, a feast of bacon, sausage, eggs, tomatoes and black pudding, often with fried (sautéed) potatoes or Boxty (page 74).

Dublin-style Pork with Apples

SERVES 4

	METRIC	IMPERIAL	AMERICAN
Butter or margarine	25 g	1 oz	2 tbsp
Large onions, chopped	2	2	2
Plain (all-purpose) flour	15 ml	1 tbsp	1 tbsp
Salt and freshly ground black pepper			
Lean pork, diced	450 g	1 lb	1 lb
Soft brown sugar	30 ml	2 tbsp	2 tbsp
Vegetable stock	300 ml	½ pt	1¼ cups
Cooking (tart) apples	4	4	4
Single (light) cream	150 ml	¼ pt	⅔ cup
Broad (fava) beans and carrots, to serve			

1 Melt the butter or margarine and fry (sauté) the onions until softened but not browned.

2 Meanwhile, season the flour with salt and pepper. Toss the meat in the seasoned flour, shaking off any excess. Add the pork to the pan and brown on all sides.

3 Stir in the sugar and stock, bring to the boil, then reduce the heat, cover and simmer gently for about 1¼ hours or until the meat is tender.

4 Peel, core and slice the apples and add to the pan. Simmer for about 15 minutes, uncovered, until the apples are just soft and the sauce has reduced.

5 Stir in the cream and heat through gently. Taste and adjust the seasoning.

6 Serve with broad beans and carrots.

🕐 **Preparation and cooking time:** 1¾ hours

Pork Cobbler

SERVES 4

	METRIC	IMPERIAL	AMERICAN
Butter or margarine	25 g	1 oz	2 tbsp
Onion, chopped	1	1	1
Carrot, chopped	1	1	1
Celery stick, chopped	1	1	1
Garlic clove, chopped	1	1	1
Lean pork, diced	450 g	1 lb	1 lb
Pigs' liver, diced	225 g	8 oz	8 oz
Chicken or vegetable stock	900 ml	1½ pts	3¾ cups
Salt and freshly ground black pepper			
Plain (all-purpose) flour	225 g	8 oz	2 cups
Baking powder	5 ml	1 tsp	1 tsp
Shredded (chopped) suet	100 g	4 oz	½ cup
Sultanas (golden raisins)	45 ml	3 tbsp	3 tbsp
Water	45 ml	3 tbsp	3 tbsp

1 Melt the butter or margarine and fry (sauté) the onion, carrot, celery and garlic until softened but not browned. Add the pork and liver and fry lightly until sealed.

2 Pour in enough stock to cover the ingredients and season to taste with salt and pepper. Bring to the boil, then reduce the heat, cover and leave to simmer gently for about 1 hour until the meat is tender.

3 Meanwhile, mix together the flour, baking powder, suet and sultanas and add a pinch of salt. Work in enough of the water to make a soft but not sticky dough. Roll out on a lightly floured surface to about 2 cm/¾ in thick and cut into rounds with a pastry (cookie) cutter.

4 Arrange the rounds over the top of the stew, cover with buttered greaseproof (waxed) paper and continue to cook for a further 1 hour until the topping is cooked.

⏱ **Preparation and cooking time:** 2¼ hours

Pork, Mushroom and Herb Pie

SERVES 4

	METRIC	IMPERIAL	AMERICAN
Butter or margarine	25 g	1 oz	2 tbsp
Onions, sliced	2	2	2
Lean pork, diced	450 g	1 lb	1 lb
Button mushrooms, halved	100 g	4 oz	4 oz
Plain (all-purpose) flour	25 g	1 oz	¼ cup
Chicken stock	300 ml	½ pt	1¼ cups
Milk	300 ml	½ pt	1¼ cups
Chopped fresh parsley	15 ml	1 tbsp	1 tbsp
Chopped fresh thyme	5 ml	1 tsp	1 tsp
Salt and freshly ground black pepper			
Puff pastry (paste)	250 g	12 oz	12 oz
Egg, lightly beaten	1	1	1

1 Melt the butter or margarine in a frying pan (skillet) and fry (sauté) the onions until softened but not browned.

2 Add the pork and fry until sealed on all sides. Add the mushrooms and stir together well. Leave to cook for about 5 minutes.

3 Sprinkle over the flour and cook for 1 minute, stirring continuously. Remove from the heat and stir in the stock and milk, then return to the heat and bring to the boil, still stirring all the time. Stir in the parsley and thyme and season to taste with salt and pepper.

4 Remove from the heat and leave to cool slightly. Place a baking (cookie) sheet in the oven and heat the oven to 200°C/400°F/gas mark 6.

5 Roll out half the pastry on a lightly floured surface and use to line a pie dish. Spoon the pork mixture into the pie dish. Roll out the remaining pastry, moisten the edges and seal to the base, trimming the edges and decorating the top with leaves cut from the trimmings. Brush with beaten egg.

6 Stand the pie dish on the hot baking sheet and bake in the preheated oven for about 40 minutes until the pastry is well risen and golden brown.

⏲ **Preparation and cooking time:** 1 hour

Boiled Bacon with Cabbage

You can use the cooking liquor for Pea and Ham Soup (page 13) if you like, but take care not to season too heavily with salt as it will already be fairly strongly flavoured.

SERVES 4

	METRIC	IMPERIAL	AMERICAN
Bacon joint, soaked overnight in cold water	900 g	2 lb	2 lb
Whole cloves	3	3	3
White cabbage	450 g	1 lb	1 lb
Freshly ground black pepper			
Boiled potatoes, to serve			

1 Drain the joint, then tie it securely and place it in a large saucepan. Pour in just enough fresh cold water to cover the joint and add the cloves. Bring to the boil, then reduce the heat, cover and simmer for 1 hour.

2 Meanwhile, trim the cabbage, cut into quarters and remove the hard core. Add to the pan, season with pepper and simmer for a further 20–30 minutes until tender but not too soft.

3 Drain and serve with boiled potatoes.

⏲ **Preparation and cooking time:** 1½ hours

Sausage and Bacon Casserole

SERVES 4–6

	METRIC	IMPERIAL	AMERICAN
Oil	15 ml	1 tbsp	1 tbsp
Pork sausages	450 g	1 lb	1 lb
Thick bacon rashers (slices), rinded and cut into chunks	450 g	1 lb	1 lb
Onion, sliced	1	1	1
Chopped fresh thyme	5 ml	1 tsp	1 tsp
Chopped fresh parsley	15 ml	1 tbsp	1 tbsp
Bay leaf	1	1	1
Salt and freshly ground black pepper			
Potatoes, thinly sliced	450 g	1 lb	1 lb
Chicken or vegetable stock	1.2 litres	2 pts	5 cups
Butter or margarine	15 g	½ oz	1 tbsp

1 Heat the oil in a large frying pan (skillet) and fry (sauté) the sausages and bacon until lightly browned. Remove from the pan.

2 Fry the onion in the same pan until just soft. Remove from the heat, stir in the bacon and sausages, add the herbs and season with salt and pepper.

3 Arrange half the potatoes in a layer on the base of a casserole dish (Dutch oven). Spoon over the sausage mixture, then top with the remaining potatoes. Pour over the stock, just up to the level of the potatoes. Press the potatoes down gently into the liquid.

4 Cook in a preheated oven at 160°C/325°F/gas mark 3 for about 2 hours until all the ingredients are cooked through and tender.

5 Dot the top with butter or margarine, increase the oven temperature to 200°C/400°F/gas mark 6 and cook for a further 20 minutes until lightly browned on top.

⏱ **Preparation and cooking time:** 2¾ hours

Limerick-style Ham in Cider

SERVES 8

	METRIC	IMPERIAL	AMERICAN
Limerick ham, soaked overnight in cold water	1.5–2.25 kg	3–5 lb	3–5 lb
Dry cider	1.75 litres	3 pts	7½ cups
Soft brown sugar	100 g	4 oz	½ cup
Mustard powder	5 ml	1 tsp	1 tsp
Whole cloves	15	15	15
Potatoes and peas, to serve			

1 Place the ham in a large saucepan, cover with fresh cold water and bring to the boil. Strain off the water, then return the meat to the pan and add enough cider to cover.

2 Bring to the boil, then reduce the heat, cover and simmer very gently for 1–1¼ hours, allowing 20 minutes per 450 g/1 lb. Turn off the heat and leave to cool in the liquid for 30 minutes, then lift out the joint.

3 Remove the skin, leaving just a thin layer of fat, and score the fat in a diamond pattern.

4 Mix together the sugar and mustard and rub all over the fat, then press in the cloves where the scores intersect.

5 Bake in a preheated oven at 200°C/400°F/gas mark 6 for 30–50 minutes (10 minutes per 450 g/1 lb), until glazed and golden.

6 Leave to cool, then slice and serve with potatoes and peas.

🕑 **Preparation and cooking time:** 1¾–2¾ hours

Dublin Coddle

SERVES 4

	METRIC	IMPERIAL	AMERICAN
Ham or vegetable stock	*300 ml*	*½ pt*	*1¼ cups*
Sausages	*450 g*	*1 lb*	*1 lb*
Thick streaky bacon rashers			
(slices), rinded and chopped	*225 g*	*8 oz*	*8 oz*
Potatoes, peeled and thickly			
sliced	*6*	*6*	*6*
Onions, sliced	*3*	*3*	*3*
Salt and freshly ground black			
pepper			

1 Bring the stock to the boil in a large, heavy-based saucepan, add the sausages and bacon, then reduce the heat and simmer for 5 minutes.

2 Remove the sausages and bacon and reserve the liquid. Cut each sausage into several chunks.

3 Starting and finishing with a layer of potatoes, layer the ingredients into the saucepan, pour over the reserved cooking liquid and season with salt and pepper. Cover and simmer gently for 1 hour until all the ingredients are tender.

⏲ **Preparation and cooking time:** 1¼ hours

Gammon Steaks with Whiskey Sauce

SERVES 4

	METRIC	IMPERIAL	AMERICAN
Gammon steaks	4	4	4
Butter or margarine	25 g	1 oz	2 tbsp
Shallots, finely chopped	2	2	2
Plain (all-purpose) flour	15 ml	1 tbsp	1 tbsp
Soft brown sugar	15 ml	1 tbsp	1 tbsp
Irish whiskey	15 ml	1 tbsp	1 tbsp
Vegetable stock	300 ml	½ pt	1¼ cups
Salt and freshly ground black pepper			
Sautéed potatoes and a green vegetable, to serve			

1 Snip the rind and fat on the steaks so that they stay flat. Dot with half the butter or margarine and grill (broil) under a hot grill (broiler) for about 8 minutes on each side until they are cooked through and the fat is crisp.

2 Meanwhile, melt the remaining butter or margarine in a small pan and fry (sauté) the shallots until softened but not browned. Stir in the flour and cook for 1 minute, then stir in the sugar until well blended.

3 Add the whiskey and stir well, then add the stock and bring to the boil. Reduce the heat, then simmer, stirring continuously, until the sauce thickens. Add a little more water if the sauce is too thick, or simmer to reduce if it is too thin. Taste and season with salt, if necessary, and pepper.

4 Arrange the steaks on a warmed serving dish, pour over the sauce and serve with sautéed potatoes and a green vegetable.

⏰ **Preparation and cooking time:** 30 minutes

Bacon and Oatmeal Pancakes

This makes about eight pancakes but you can make smaller or larger pancakes if you prefer.

SERVES 4

	METRIC	IMPERIAL	AMERICAN
Plain (all-purpose) flour	100 g	4 oz	1 cup
Fine oatmeal	25 g	1 oz	2 tbsp
A pinch of salt			
Egg, beaten	1	1	1
Milk or buttermilk	150 ml	¼ pt	⅔ cup
Streaky bacon rashers (slices), rinded	8	8	8
A little oil			
Made mild mustard	15 ml	1 tbsp	1 tbsp

1 Whisk together the flour, oatmeal, salt, egg and milk or buttermilk to make a thick batter.

2 Grill (broil) the bacon until crisp.

3 Heat a little oil in a medium-sized frying pan (skillet) and pour in enough batter to cover the base of the pan. Cook for about 2 minutes until the underside is golden, then turn the pancake over and cook for 1 minute.

4 Spread the top with a little mustard, lay a bacon rasher across the pancake and fold the pancake in half. Remove it from the pan and keep it warm while you cook the remaining pancakes in the same way.

⏱ **Preparation and cooking time:** 20 minutes

Apple Jelly

I have placed this recipe in this meat section as the jelly (clear conserve) makes a perfect accompaniment to pork. However, it is just as delicious with scones (biscuits), bread or pancakes.

MAKES ABOUT 2.25 KG/5 LB

	METRIC	IMPERIAL	AMERICAN
Cooking (tart) apples	2 kg	5 lb	5 lb
Water	2 litres	3½ pts	8½ cups
Whole cloves	10	10	10
Preserving sugar	1.75 kg	4 lb	8 cups

1 Wash the apples thoroughly but do not peel or core them. Chop them and place them in a preserving pan or large saucepan. Add the water and cloves and bring to the boil. Reduce the heat, then cover and simmer for about 1 hour until the apples are very mushy.

2 Suspend a jelly bag over a large saucepan and spoon the cooked apples into the bag. Leave to stand for several hours until all the juice has dripped through. Do not squeeze the bag or the jelly will be cloudy.

3 Measure the liquid and for every 600 ml/1 pt/2½ cups of liquid, add 450g/1 lb/2 cups of sugar. Bring slowly to the boil, stirring occasionally until the sugar has dissolved, then boil rapidly for about 10 minutes until setting point is reached. (To test for setting point, place a teaspoonful of the jelly on a cold saucer. If the cool mixture wrinkles when pressed, it has reached setting point.)

4 Pour into warmed jars and leave until cold, then cover and store in a cool place.

⊘ **Preparation and cooking time:** 2 hours plus standing

Poultry and Game

A ll Irish farms kept chickens in the yard, and many still do, but even if you live in an urban apartment, chickens are among the most readily available of ingredients. Choose corn-fed or free-range organic chickens; it is worth paying a little more to get the best flavour.

Irish Chicken Pot-roast

SERVES 4

	METRIC	IMPERIAL	AMERICAN
Chicken, about 1.5 kg/3 lb	1	1	1
Salt and freshly ground black pepper			
Onions	4	4	4
Medium oatmeal	100 ml	4 oz	1 cup
Shredded (chopped) suet	25 g	1 oz	2 tbsp
Chicken stock	500 ml	17 fl oz	2¼ cups
Oil or lard (shortening)	25 g	1 oz	2 tbsp
Thick streaky bacon rashers (slices), rinded and chopped	175 g	6 oz	6 oz
Carrots, sliced	3	3	3
Potatoes, thickly sliced	900 g	2 lb	2 lb
Plain (all-purpose) flour	30 ml	2 tbsp	2 tbsp

1 Season the chicken inside and out with salt and pepper.

2 Chop one of the onions and mix with the oatmeal, suet and 45 ml/3 tbsp of the chicken stock. Season with salt and pepper and stuff into the chicken.

3 Slice the three remaining onions, then heat the oil or lard and fry (sauté) the sliced onions with the bacon and carrots until softened but not browned. Transfer them to a casserole dish (Dutch oven).

4 Brown the chicken in the same fat, then place on top of the vegetables.

5 Cook the potatoes in boiling salted water for about 5 minutes, then drain. Toss in the flour, then add to the casserole and pour over the remaining stock. Season with salt and pepper.

6 Cover and cook in a preheated oven at 180°C/350°F/ gas mark 4 for about 1 hour until the chicken is well cooked, removing the lid for the last 15 minutes to brown the chicken.

☺ **Preparation and cooking time:** 1¼ hours

Roast Chicken with Mashed Potato Stuffing

You can also use this stuffing for roast goose. Allow at least an extra 30 minutes' cooking time.

SERVES 4

	METRIC	IMPERIAL	AMERICAN
Butter or margarine	25 g	1 oz	2 tbsp
Onions, chopped	2	2	2
Bacon rashers (slices), rinded and chopped	2	2	2
Mushrooms, roughly chopped	100 g	4 oz	4 oz
Chopped fresh thyme	5 ml	1 tsp	1 tsp
Salt and freshly ground black pepper			
Mashed potatoes	225 g	8 oz	8 oz
Egg, lightly beaten	1	1	1
Chicken, about 1.5 kg/3 lb	1	1	1
Cornflour (cornstarch)	10 ml	2 tsp	2 tsp
Chicken stock	300 ml	½ pt	1¼ cups
Seasonal vegetables, to serve			

1 Melt the butter or margarine in a heavy-based frying pan (skillet) and fry (sauté) the onions and bacon until softened but not browned. Stir in the mushrooms and cook for 3 minutes. Season with thyme, salt and pepper.

2 Spoon the mixture, including the cooking fat, into the mashed potatoes and blend together well. Add the egg and mix to bind.

3 Stuff the chicken with the potato stuffing, place in a flameproof roasting tin (pan) and roast in a preheated oven at 200°C/400°F/gas mark 6 for 20 minutes. Reduce the oven temperature to 190°C/375°F/gas mark 5 and roast for a further 1 hour or until the juices run clear from the thickest part of the thigh when pierced with a skewer.

4 Remove the chicken from the pan, cover with foil and leave to rest.

5 Pour off any excess fat from the pan and stir the cornflour into the juices. Cook over a low heat for 1 minute. Add the stock, bring to the boil, then reduce the heat and simmer for 4 minutes, stirring regularly, to make a gravy.

6 Carve the chicken, then serve with seasonal vegetables and the gravy offered separately.

🕐 **Preparation and cooking time:** 1¾ hours

Rabbit Casserole in Milk

SERVES 4

	METRIC	IMPERIAL	AMERICAN
Rabbit, jointed	1	1	1
Juice of 1 lemon			
Plain (all-purpose) flour	30 ml	2 tbsp	2 tbsp
Mustard powder	2.5 ml	½ tsp	½ tsp
Salt and freshly ground black pepper			
Lard (shortening) or vegetable fat	15 ml	1 tbsp	1 tbsp
Onions, chopped	2	2	2
Carrot, chopped	1	1	1
Celery stick, chopped	1	1	1
Bacon rashers (slices), rinded and chopped	5	5	5
Milk	300 ml	½ pt	1¼ cups
Chopped fresh mixed herbs	15 ml	1 tbsp	1 tbsp
Boiled potatoes and seasonal vegetables, to serve			

1 Place the rabbit joints in a bowl, squeeze over the lemon juice and add enough water to cover. Leave to soak for 1 hour, then drain and pat dry on kitchen paper (paper towels).

2 Season the flour generously with mustard, salt and pepper. Toss the joints in the flour, shaking off any excess.

3 Melt the lard or vegetable fat in a flameproof casserole dish (Dutch oven) and fry (sauté) the lamb joints until browned. Remove from the dish.

4 Add the onions, carrot, celery and bacon and fry until softened but not browned. Add the milk and herbs and bring to the boil. Remove from the heat, return the rabbit to the pan and season to taste with salt and pepper.

5 Cover and cook in a preheated oven at 180°C/350°F/ gas mark 4 for 1 hour until the rabbit is tender.

6 Serve with boiled potatoes and seasonal vegetables.

🕐 **Preparation and cooking time:** 1¼ hours plus soaking

Chicken and Leek Pie

SERVES 4

	METRIC	IMPERIAL	AMERICAN
Boned chicken, diced	450 g	1 lb	1 lb
Ham, diced	100 g	4 oz	4 oz
Leeks, cut into chunks	4	4	4
Shallots, chopped	3	3	3
Ground mace	2.5 ml	½ tsp	½ tsp
Salt and freshly ground black pepper			
Chicken stock	300 ml	½ pt	1¼ cups
Single (light) cream	150 ml	¼ pt	⅔ cup
Shortcrust pastry (basic pie crust)	175 g	6 oz	6 oz
A little milk, to glaze			

1 Layer the chicken, ham, leeks and shallots in a pie dish. Season with mace, salt and pepper. Mix together the stock and cream and pour over the ingredients.

2 Roll out the pastry (paste) on a lightly floured surface and use to cover the pie, moistening and sealing the edges to the dish. Decorate with the pastry trimmings and brush with milk.

3 Bake in a preheated oven at 190°C/375°F/gas mark 5 for about 35 minutes until cooked through and golden. Cover with greaseproof (waxed) paper for the last 10 minutes if the pastry is becoming too brown.

🕐 **Preparation and cooking time:** 45 minutes

Rabbit with Sweet Herb Stuffing

SERVES 4

	METRIC	IMPERIAL	AMERICAN
Butter or margarine	75 g	3 oz	⅓ cup
Onion, chopped	1	1	1
Cooking (tart) apples, peeled, cored and chopped	2	2	2
Chopped fresh parsley	10 ml	2 tsp	2 tsp
Chopped fresh thyme	5 ml	1 tsp	1 tsp
Chopped fresh sage	5 ml	1 tsp	1 tsp
Fresh wholemeal breadcrumbs	100 g	4 oz	2 cups
Soft brown sugar	15 ml	1 tbsp	1 tbsp
Salt and freshly ground black pepper			
Egg, lightly beaten	1	1	1
Rabbit	1	1	1
Plain (all-purpose) flour	25 g	1 oz	¼ cup
Rabbit, chicken or vegetable stock	300 ml	½ pt	1¼ cups
Roast potatoes and parsnips, to serve			

1 Melt 50 g/2 oz/¼ cup of the butter or margarine and fry (sauté) the onion until softened but not browned. Add the cooking apples and fry together, stirring until softened and well mixed. Stir in the herbs.

2 Remove from the pan with a slotted spoon and stir in the breadcrumbs. Add the sugar, season to taste with salt and pepper and mix in the egg to bind.

3 Fill the rabbit with the stuffing and secure with string.

4 Season the flour with salt and pepper, then dust the rabbit with the flour. Add the remaining butter or margarine to the pan and fry the rabbit on all sides until sealed and just browned all over. Transfer to a casserole dish (Dutch oven) and pour over the stock.

5 Cover and cook in a preheated oven at 180°C/350°F/gas mark 4 for about 2 hours until the rabbit is very tender.

6 Serve with roast potatoes and parsnips.

🕐 **Preparation and cooking time:** 2½ hours

Roast Venison

The traditional Irish method is to wrap the joint in greaseproof (waxed) paper, cover it with a thick flour and water paste and then another layer of greaseproof. This seals in all the flavours while the joint is roasting.

SERVES 4-6

	METRIC	IMPERIAL	AMERICAN
Venison joint	900 g	2 lb	2 lb
Onions, chopped	2	2	2
Carrot, chopped	1	1	1
Garlic clove, chopped	1	1	1
Chopped fresh parsley	30 ml	2 tbsp	2 tbsp
Chopped fresh thyme	15 ml	1 tbsp	1 tbsp
Bay leaf	1	1	1
Black peppercorns	6	6	6
Coriander (cilantro) seeds	8	8	8
Juniper berries	6	6	6
Grated rind and juice of 1 lemon			
Red wine	600 ml	1 pt	2½ cups
Oil	150 ml	¼ pt	⅔ cup
Soft brown sugar	30 ml	2 tbsp	2 tbsp
Butter or margarine	50 g	2 oz	¼ cup
Roast potatoes, gravy, carrots and redcurrant jelly (clear conserve), to serve			

1 Place the joint in an earthenware casserole dish (Dutch oven). Mix together all the remaining ingredients except the butter or margarine, pour over the joint and leave to marinate in a cool place for 24–48 hours, turning and basting occasionally. The longer you marinate the meat, the stronger the flavour will be.

2 Remove the joint from the marinade and pat dry on kitchen paper (paper towels). Wrap in a double thickness of foil and seal securely at the top.

3 Roast in a preheated oven at 180°C/350°F/gas mark 4 for 1 hour. Remove the foil and return to the oven for a further 15 minutes to finish.

4 Slice the meat and serve hot with roast potatoes, gravy, carrots and redcurrant jelly.

⊙ **Preparation and cooking time:** 1½ hours plus marinating

Roast Duck

SERVES 2

	METRIC	IMPERIAL	AMERICAN
Duck, about 1.75 kg/4 lb	1	1	1
Salt and freshly ground black pepper			
Shallots	4	4	4
Whole cloves	4	4	4
Streaky bacon rashers (slices), rinded	4	4	4
Plain (all-purpose) flour	15 ml	1 tbsp	1 tbsp
Chicken stock	300 ml	½ pt	1¼ cups
Sautéed potatoes and peas, to serve			

1 Place the duck on a rack over the sink and pour over a kettleful of boiling water. Leave to drain, then pat dry on kitchen paper (paper towels). Season the duck inside and out.

2 Stud the shallots with the cloves and place inside the duck cavity. Place the duck on a rack in a roasting tin (pan) and stretch the bacon rashers over the top.

3 Roast in a preheated oven at 220°C/425°F/gas mark 7 for 10 minutes, then reduce the oven temperature to 180°C/350°F/gas mark 4 and continue to roast for a further 1 hour until the duck is tender.

4 Remove the duck from the pan, cover with foil and leave to rest.

5 Pour off the fat from the pan, stir the flour into the roasting juices and cook on the hob for 1 minute until blended, stirring continuously. Stir or whisk in the stock, bring to the boil, then reduce the heat and simmer for about 5 minutes until you have a thick gravy. Season to taste.

6 Carve the duck and serve with sautéed potatoes and peas, with the gravy handed separately.

⊙ **Preparation and cooking time:** 1½ hours

Fish and Seafood

As an island nation with a network of clear rivers and lakes, Ireland enjoys a plentiful source of fish and seafood of all kinds. In fact, many early settlements began around the coast, where fish formed the basis of the people's diet. For fish straight out of the sea, one of the best cooking methods is simply to grill (broil) it and serve it with new or boiled potatoes and plenty of fresh Irish butter.

Cod with Cheese Scones

SERVES 4

	METRIC	IMPERIAL	AMERICAN
Cod or other white fish fillets, skinned and cut into large pieces	450 g	1 lb	1 lb
Salt and freshly ground black pepper			
Butter or margarine	50 g	2 oz	¼ cup
Plain (all-purpose) flour	50 g	2 oz	½ cup
Milk	600 ml	1 pt	2½ cups
Cheddar cheese, grated	50 g	2 oz	½ cup
For the scones (biscuits):			
Plain (all-purpose) flour	225 g	8 oz	2 cups
Baking powder	5 ml	1 tsp	1 tsp
Butter or margarine	50 g	2 oz	¼ cup
Cheddar cheese, grated	100 g	4 oz	½ cup
Egg, lightly beaten	1	1	1
Milk (optional)	15–45 ml	1–3 tbsp	1–3 tbsp
Parmesan cheese, freshly grated	25 g	1 oz	¼ cup

1 Arrange the fish fillets in the base of a greased ovenproof dish and season with salt and pepper.

2 Melt the butter or margarine in a saucepan, then stir in the flour and cook for 1 minute, stirring continuously. Remove from the heat and whisk in the milk, then return to the heat and stir until the mixture boils and thickens. Continue to cook for 3 minutes, stirring. Remove from the heat, stir in the cheese and season with salt and pepper. Pour over the fish.

3 To make the scones, place the flour and baking powder in a bowl and add a pinch of salt. Rub in the butter or margarine until the mixture resembles breadcrumbs. Stir in the Cheddar cheese. Add the egg and enough of the milk to make a smooth but not sticky dough.

4 Roll out on a lightly floured surface to 1 cm/½ in thick and cut into rounds with a 5 cm/2 in pastry (cookie) cutter.

5 Arrange the scones on top of the fish, brush with a little milk and sprinkle with the Parmesan.

6 Bake in a preheated oven at 200°C/400°F/gas mark 6 for 25–30 minutes until cooked through and golden brown on top.

⏲ **Preparation and cooking time:** 40–45 minutes

Dublin Bay Prawns in Whiskey Cream

SERVES 4

	METRIC	IMPERIAL	AMERICAN
Butter or margarine	25 g	1 oz	2 tbsp
Dublin Bay prawns (shrimp), cooked and peeled	450 g	1 lb	1 lb
Irish whiskey	45 ml	3 tbsp	3 tbsp
Single (light) cream	150 ml	¼ pt	⅔ cup
Salt and freshly ground black pepper			
Boiled rice or new potatoes, to serve			

1 Melt the butter or margarine in a large frying pan (skillet), add the prawns and stir together quickly until coated in butter.

2 Add the whiskey and cook for 1 minute to evaporate the alcohol.

3 Add the cream, season with salt and pepper, then heat through quickly before serving with boiled rice or new potatoes.

⏲ **Preparation and cooking time:** 10 minutes

Galway Cod with Cockles

SERVES 4

	METRIC	IMPERIAL	AMERICAN
Cockles, scrubbed	24	24	24
Potatoes, peeled and quartered	450 g	1 lb	1 lb
Shallots	8	8	8
Cod steaks, 175 g/6 oz each	4	4	4
Salt and freshly ground black pepper			
Sprigs of thyme	2	2	2
Butter or margarine	25 g	1 oz	2 tbsp
Chopped fresh parsley	15 ml	1 tbsp	1 tbsp
A few slices of lemon			

1 Place the cockles in a heavy-based saucepan with just enough water to cover them, put on a lid and place over a heat for about 4 minutes, shaking the pan occasionally until all the shells have opened. Strain, reserving the cooking liquid, and discard any shells that have not opened. Remove the cockles from their shells.

2 Meanwhile, boil the potatoes and shallots for about 8 minutes until part-cooked, then drain well.

3 Arrange the cod steaks in the base of a greased, shallow ovenproof dish, surround with the potatoes and shallots and top with the cockles. Season with salt and pepper, add the thyme and dot with butter or margarine. Spoon over enough of the reserved cooking liquid to moisten the fish, then cover with kitchen foil.

4 Bake in a preheated oven at 200°C/400°F/gas mark 6 for about 25 minutes until the cod is tender and the vegetables are cooked. Discard the sprigs of thyme.

5 Serve sprinkled with parsley and garnished with lemon slices.

🕐 **Preparation and cooking time:** 40 minutes

Herrings in Oatmeal with Red Apples

You can clean and descale the herrings yourself if you prefer, but it is a very messy job, so I prefer to ask my fishmonger to do it for me!

SERVES 4

	METRIC	IMPERIAL	AMERICAN
Herrings, cleaned	4	4	4
Plain (all-purpose) flour	15 ml	1 tbsp	1 tbsp
Salt and freshly ground black pepper			
Egg, beaten	1	1	1
Medium oatmeal	50 g	2 oz	½ cup
Oil	45 ml	3 tbsp	3 tbsp
Red eating (dessert) apples, cored and sliced into rings	2	2	2
A few sprigs of parsley			

1 Remove the heads, tails and fins from the herrings. Season the flour with salt and pepper, then toss the fish in the flour, shaking off any excess.

2 Dip the herrings in beaten egg, then coat with oatmeal.

3 Heat the oil in a heavy-based frying pan (skillet) and fry (sauté) the herrings for about 5 minutes on each side. Remove from the pan and drain on kitchen paper (paper towels). Keep hot.

4 Add the apple slices to the hot pan and fry for a few seconds until just golden, turning once.

5 Arrange the herrings on a warmed serving plate, top with the apple slices and garnish with parsley sprigs. Serve at once.

🕐 **Preparation and cooking time:** 25 minutes

Stuffed Herrings in Cider

SERVES 4

	METRIC	IMPERIAL	AMERICAN
Fresh wholemeal breadcrumbs	50 g	2 oz	1 cup
Chopped fresh parsley	15 ml	1 tbsp	1 tbsp
Chopped fresh thyme	5 ml	1 tsp	1 tsp
Grated rind and juice of 1 lemon			
Egg, lightly beaten	1	1	1
Grated nutmeg	2.5 ml	½ tsp	½ tsp
Salt and freshly ground black pepper			
Herrings, cleaned	4	4	4
Dry cider	300 ml	½ pt	1¼ cups
Bay leaf	1	1	1
Creamy Apple Mashed Potatoes (page 73) and peas, to serve			

1 Mix together the breadcrumbs, parsley, thyme, lemon rind and juice, egg and nutmeg and season with salt and pepper.

2 Season the fish with salt and pepper, then fill the cavities with the stuffing. Arrange the fish in a single layer in an ovenproof dish. Pour over the cider, add the bay leaf and cover with foil.

3 Bake in a preheated oven at 180°C/350°F/gas mark 4 for about 35 minutes until the fish flakes easily when tested with a fork.

4 Serve with Creamy Apple Mashed Potatoes and peas.

🕐 **Preparation and cooking time:** 45 minutes

Potted Herring

SERVES 4

	METRIC	IMPERIAL	AMERICAN
Herrings, cleaned	6	6	6
Sea salt			
Onion, sliced	1	1	1
Bay leaves	4	4	4
Pickling spice	5 ml	1 tsp	1 tsp
Malt vinegar	150 ml	¼ pt	⅔ cup
Water	150 ml	¼ pt	⅔ cup
Soda Bread (page 106), to serve			

1 Remove the heads, tails and fins from the herrings. Rub them with sea salt and place in an ovenproof dish. Add the onion, bay leaves and pickling spice.

2 Mix together the vinegar and water and pour over the fish so that they are just covered. Cover and cook in a preheated oven at 160°C/325°F/gas mark 3 for 40 minutes until the herrings are tender. Remove from the oven, take off the lid and leave the herrings to cool in the liquid.

3 Serve with a little of the liquid and plenty of soda bread.

🕐 **Preparation and cooking time:** 45 minutes plus cooling

Dublin Lawyer

*Many cooks maintain that you can only appreciate the flavour if you
use a fresh, live lobster, which you kill by plunging a sharp knife into
the cross on the back of the shell. However, I prefer to buy a very
freshly cooked lobster. To remove the meat from a raw or cooked
lobster, twist off the legs and claws, crack them open and extract the
meat. Using a large, sharp knife, split the lobster in half down the
back of the head and then along the centre of the back. Remove the
gills from behind the head and the black intestine, which runs down
the length of the body. As well as the meat, the red coral, any black
roe and the green tomalley are all edible.*

SERVES 2

	METRIC	IMPERIAL	AMERICAN
Unsalted (sweet) butter	100 g	4 oz	½ cup
Lobster meat	450 g	1 lb	1 lb
Irish whiskey	120 ml	4 fl oz	½ cup
Double (heavy) cream	150 ml	¼ pt	⅔ cup
Salt and freshly ground black pepper			
New potatoes and green beans, to serve			

1 Heat the butter in a heavy-based frying pan (skillet)
until foaming, then add the lobster meat and toss over a
medium heat for 4–5 minutes until cooked, making sure the
butter does not burn.

2 Pour over the whiskey and heat until it has warmed
through, then set light to it and leave until the flames die
down.

3 Gently stir in the cream and heat through, then season
to taste before serving with new potatoes and green beans.

🕐 **Preparation and cooking time:** 15 minutes

Grilled Mustard Mackerel

SERVES 4

	METRIC	IMPERIAL	AMERICAN
Mackerel, cleaned	4	4	4
Made mustard	30 ml	2 tbsp	2 tbsp
Salt and freshly ground black pepper			
Butter or margarine	25 g	1 oz	2 tbsp
A few sprigs of parsley			
Boiled potatoes and peas, to serve			

1 Cut the heads and tails off the mackerel and trim off the fins. Make three diagonal slashes across each side of the fish. Rub the mustard into the cuts and season the fish inside and out with salt and pepper.

2 Place on a grill (broiler) pan and dot with half the butter or margarine. Grill (broil) under a medium grill for about 10 minutes until the skin is crisp, then turn them over, dot with the remaining butter or margarine and grill for a further 5 minutes until the skin is crisp and the fish cooked through.

3 Garnish with sprigs of parsley and serve with boiled potatoes and peas.

🕐 **Preparation and cooking time:** 20 minutes

Mackerel with Rhubarb

SERVES 4

	METRIC	IMPERIAL	AMERICAN
Butter or margarine	75 g	3 oz	⅓ cup
Onion, chopped	1	1	1
Rhubarb, chopped	700 g	1½ lb	1½ lb
Fresh white breadcrumbs	50 g	2 oz	1 cup
Salt and freshly ground black pepper			
Mackerel, filleted	4	4	4
Caster (superfine) sugar	50 g	2 oz	¼ cup
Grated rind of 1 lemon			

1 Melt half the butter or margarine and fry (sauté) the onion until softened but not browned. Add 225 g/8 oz of the rhubarb and cook for 5 minutes, stirring occasionally. Stir in the breadcrumbs and season with salt and pepper.

2 Lay the mackerel fillets out flat, skin-side down, on a work surface. Cover with the stuffing, then roll them up and secure with cocktail sticks (toothpicks). Arrange fairly tightly in a greased, ovenproof dish and dot with the remaining butter or margarine.

3 Bake in a preheated oven at 200°C/400°/gas mark 6 for 20 minutes until cooked through.

4 Meanwhile, rinse the remaining rhubarb and place in a saucepan with only the water clinging to the fruit. Add the sugar and lemon rind and simmer gently for about 10 minutes until tender.

5 Purée in a food processor or blender to make a sauce. Serve hot or cold with the mackerel.

🕐 **Preparation and cooking time:** 35 minutes

Monkfish with Garlic Butter

SERVES 4

	METRIC	IMPERIAL	AMERICAN
Garlic cloves, crushed	2–3	2–3	2–3
Chopped fresh parsley	15 ml	1 tbsp	1 tbsp
Butter or margarine, softened	100 g	4 oz	½ cup
Monkfish fillets	450 g	1 lb	1 lb
Plain (all-purpose) flour	15 ml	1 tbsp	1 tbsp
Salt and freshly ground black pepper			
Egg, beaten	1	1	1
Fresh white breadcrumbs	100 g	4 oz	2 cups
Lemon slices, to garnish			

1 Blend 1–2 cloves of garlic and the parsley into 75 g/ 3 oz/⅓ cup of the butter or margarine, using enough garlic to flavour the butter to your liking. Wrap in clingfilm (plastic wrap) and chill.

2 Cut the monkfish fillets into large chunks. Season the flour with salt and pepper and toss the fish in the flour, shaking off any excess. Dip the fish in the egg, then coat in breadcrumbs.

3 Melt the remaining butter or margarine in a heavy-based frying pan (skillet) and add the remaining garlic.

4 Fry (sauté) the fish for about 20 minutes until golden on both sides.

5 Arrange on a warmed serving plate, top with the garlic butter and serve garnished with lemon slices.

⊘ **Preparation and cooking time:** 35 minutes

Mussels in Lemon Butter

You can make Oysters in Lemon Butter, using the same method.

SERVES 4

	METRIC	IMPERIAL	AMERICAN
Mussels, scrubbed and bearded	1.2 litres	2 pts	5 cups
Juice of 1 lemon			
Water	150 ml	¼ pt	⅔ cup
Butter or margarine	100 g	4 oz	½ cup
Salt and freshly ground black pepper			
Snipped fresh chives	30 ml	2 tbsp	2 tbsp
Wholemeal bread and butter, to serve			

1 Place the mussels, lemon juice and water in a large saucepan and bring to the boil. Cover and shake over a high heat for about 5 minutes until all the shells have opened; discard any that remain closed.

2 Strain, reserving the cooking liquor, and arrange the mussels in a warmed serving dish. Strain the liquor again through a fine sieve (strainer) or muslin (cheesecloth).

3 Add the butter or margarine to the saucepan and heat until melted, then whisk in the cooking liquor and heat through. Taste and adjust the seasoning, if necessary. Pour over the mussels, sprinkle with chives and serve at once with wholemeal bread and butter.

⊘ **Preparation and cooking time:** 15 minutes

Baked Plaice with Soured Cream and Chives

SERVES 4

	METRIC	IMPERIAL	AMERICAN
Plaice fillets	*4*	*4*	*4*
Milk	*15 ml*	*1 tbsp*	*1 tbsp*
Butter or margarine	*50 g*	*2 oz*	*¼ cup*
Salt and freshly ground black pepper			
Soured (dairy sour) cream	*150 ml*	*¼ pt*	*⅔ cup*
Snipped fresh chives	*15 ml*	*1 tbsp*	*1 tbsp*
Mashed potatoes and peas, to serve			

1 Arrange the plaice in an ovenproof dish, spoon over the milk and dot with butter or margarine. Season with salt and pepper.

2 Cover tightly with foil or a lid and bake in a preheated oven at 160°C/325°F/gas mark 3 for 30 minutes until the fish flakes easily when tested with a fork.

3 Transfer the fish to a warmed serving plate. Stir the soured cream and chives into the ovenproof dish and warm through gently, then pour over the fish and serve with mashed potatoes and peas.

🕐 **Preparation and cooking time:** 40 minutes

Baked Salmon in Wine

SERVES 4

	METRIC	IMPERIAL	AMERICAN
Salmon, about 1.75 kg/4 lb, cleaned	1	1	1
Salt and freshly ground black pepper			
A handful of fresh parsley			
Unsalted (sweet) butter	100 g	4 oz	½ cup
Dry white wine or cider	120 ml	4 fl oz	½ cup
Double (heavy) cream	300 ml	½ pt	1¼ cups
New potatoes and seasonal vegetables, to serve			

1 Remove the head, tail and fins from the salmon. Season with salt and pepper. Stuff the parsley into the cavity.

2 Dot some of the butter over a large piece of foil, place the fish on top and dot with the remaining butter. Shape the foil around the fish, pour over the wine or cider and cream and season with salt and pepper. Seal into a loose parcel, allowing plenty of space above the fish.

3 Bake in a preheated oven at 180°C/350°F/gas mark 4 for about 1¼ hours until the salmon flakes when tested with a fork.

4 Lift the salmon on to a warmed serving plate. Pour off the cooking liquor into a small saucepan and boil until reduced by half, then pour it back over the salmon and serve with new potatoes and seasonal vegetables.

⏰ **Preparation and cooking time:** 1½ hours

Trout with Herb Stuffing

SERVES 4

	METRIC	IMPERIAL	AMERICAN
Butter or margarine	25 g	1 oz	2 tbsp
Shallots, chopped	2	2	2
Fresh wholemeal breadcrumbs	50 g	2 oz	1 cup
Chopped fresh parsley	15 ml	1 tbsp	1 tbsp
Grated lemon rind	2.5 ml	½ tsp	½ tsp
Salt and freshly ground black pepper			
Egg, lightly beaten	1	1	1
Brown or rainbow trout, cleaned	4	4	4
New potatoes and a green vegetable, to serve			

1 Melt half the butter or margarine and fry (sauté) the shallots until softened but not browned. Remove from the heat and stir in the breadcrumbs, parsley and lemon rind and season with salt and pepper. Leave to cool slightly, then stir in enough of the egg to bind the stuffing ingredients together.

2 Season the fish inside and out with salt and pepper, then fill with the stuffing mixture. Arrange in a single layer in a greased ovenproof dish and dot with the remaining butter.

3 Bake in a preheated oven at 200°C/400°F/gas mark 6 for about 25 minutes until the fish flakes easily when tested with a fork.

4 Serve with new potatoes and a green vegetable.

⏲ **Preparation and cooking time:** 40 minutes

Scallop and Fish Pie

SERVES 4

	METRIC	IMPERIAL	AMERICAN
Scallops	4	4	4
Cod or haddock, skinned and cut into chunks	450 g	1 lb	1 lb
Onion, chopped	1	1	1
Bouquet garni sachet	1	1	1
Freshly ground black pepper			
Milk	450 ml	¾ pt	2 cups
Potatoes, peeled and quartered	450 g	1 lb	1 lb
Butter or margarine	50 g	2 oz	¼ cup
Salt			
Mushrooms, sliced	100 g	4 oz	4 oz
Plain (all-purpose) flour	15 ml	1 tbsp	1 tbsp
Single (light) cream	60 ml	4 tbsp	4 tbsp
Dry sherry	15 ml	1 tbsp	1 tbsp
Seasonal vegetables, to serve			

1 Separate the red corals set aside. Cut the white scallops into thick slices and place in a saucepan with the cod or haddock, onion and bouquet garni and season with pepper. Pour over 300 ml/l½ pt/1¼ cups of the milk, bring to the boil, then reduce the heat and simmer gently for 10 minutes. Add the corals and simmer for a further 3 minutes.

2 Discard the bouquet garni. Drain the fish, reserving the liquid.

3 Meanwhile, cook the potatoes in boiling salted water until tender, then drain and mash with the remaining milk and half the butter or margarine. Season to taste with salt and pepper.

4 Melt the remaining butter or margarine and fry (sauté) the mushrooms until soft. Stir in the flour and cook for 1 minute. Stir in the reserved liquid, bring to the boil, then reduce the heat and simmer for 2–3 minutes, stirring until thickened.

5 Stir in the cream and sherry and season to taste with salt and pepper. Stir in the scallops and the cod. Spoon into a greased ovenproof dish and top with the potatoes.

6 Bake in a preheated oven at 190°C/375°F/gas mark 5 for 20 minutes until golden brown.

7 Serve with seasonal vegetables.

🕐 **Preparation and cooking time:** 45 minutes

Vegetables

Many Irish people still grow their own vegetables, and so can cook with the freshest of produce, from garlic and turnips to onions and greens. Top of the list of vegetables for any collection of Irish recipes is, of course, the potato, and it is included in many delicious recipes in all sections of this book. But you'll also find plenty of other vegetables – such as peas, Brussels sprouts and parsnips – that have become somewhat unfashionable but still offer some interesting culinary options. One simple but popular Irish way of serving root vegetables is to parboil them, then finish by frying (sautéeing) them in bacon fat until crisp and golden.

Creamy Apple Mashed Potatoes

This is a rich dish that goes particularly well with strongly flavoured meats such as pork or ham. You can also use the same recipe to make Creamy Mashed Potato – just omit the apples and increase all the quantities slightly to serve four people.

SERVES 4

	METRIC	IMPERIAL	AMERICAN
Floury potatoes	*900 g*	*2 lb*	*2 lb*
Cooking (tart) apples, peeled, cored and chopped	*2*	*2*	*2*
Caster (superfine) sugar	*15 ml*	*1 tbsp*	*1 tbsp*
Butter or margarine	*50 g*	*2 oz*	*¼ cup*
Single (light) cream	*45 ml*	*3 tbsp*	*3 tbsp*
Salt and freshly ground black pepper			

1 Cook the potatoes in boiling salted water until tender, then drain and mash.

2 Meanwhile, rinse the chopped apples and place in a saucepan with only the water clinging to them. Add the sugar, bring to the boil, then reduce the heat and simmer for about 10 minutes until soft.

3 Mix together the potatoes and apples, then blend in the butter or margarine and cream. Season to taste with salt and pepper.

⊙ **Preparation and cooking time:** 30 minutes

Boxty

One of the most traditional of Irish potato recipes, Boxty can be served on its own or as part of an Irish farmhouse breakfast with bacon and black pudding, sausages and eggs. A famous Irish rhyme demonstrates the importance once given to the dish by the traditional Irish cook:

Boxty on the griddle,
Boxty in the pan,
If you can't make boxty,
You'll never get a man!

SERVES 4

	METRIC	IMPERIAL	AMERICAN
Potatoes, peeled and grated	225 g	8 oz	1 cup
Mashed potato	225 g	8 oz	1 cup
Plain (all-purpose) flour	100 g	4 oz	1 cup
Baking powder	2.5 ml	½ tsp	½ tsp
Salt and freshly ground black pepper			
Egg, lightly beaten	1	1	1
Milk	60 ml	4 tbsp	4 tbsp
A little butter or margarine			
Butter or apple sauce, to serve			

1 Mix together the grated and mashed potatoes, flour and baking powder and season with salt and pepper.

2 Work in the egg, then enough of the milk to make a soft dough.

3 Melt a little butter or margarine on a hot griddle or heavy-based frying pan (skillet) and drop in spoonfuls of the dough. Fry (sauté) over a medium heat for about 2 minutes until browned on the underside, then flip over and brown on the other side.

4 Serve with butter or apple sauce.

⏱ **Preparation and cooking time:** 15 minutes

Slim

These potato cakes make a delicious snack or part of a hearty breakfast when fried (sautéed) in butter or bacon fat.

SERVES 4

	METRIC	IMPERIAL	AMERICAN
Potatoes	450 g	1 lb	1 lb
Butter or margarine	50 g	2 oz	¼ cup
Salt and freshly ground black pepper			
Plain (all-purpose) flour	150 g	5 oz	1¼ cups
Baking powder	5 ml	1 tsp	1 tsp
Milk	30 ml	2 tbsp	2 tbsp
Egg, lightly beaten			
Butter, to serve			

1 Cook the potatoes in boiling salted water until tender, then drain and mash with the butter or margarine and salt and pepper to taste.

2 Gradually beat in the flour, baking powder and milk to make a soft dough.

3 Roll out on a lightly floured surface to about 1 cm/½ in thick and cut into 5 cm/2 in rounds with a pastry (cookie) cutter.

4 Brush with beaten egg and arrange on a greased baking (cookie) sheet.

5 Bake in a preheated oven at 225°C/450°F/gas mark 7 for 15 minutes until golden, or cook on a greased griddle or heavy-based frying pan (skillet) until golden on both sides.

6 Serve with plenty of butter.

⊙ **Preparation and cooking time:** 30 minutes

Champ

Use both the green and white parts of the spring onions (scallions) for this recipe.

SERVES 4

	METRIC	IMPERIAL	AMERICAN
Potatoes	*450 g*	*1 lb*	*1 lb*
Bunch of spring onions (scallions), chopped	*1*	*1*	*1*
Milk	*150 ml*	*¼ pt*	*⅔ cup*
Salt and freshly ground black pepper			
Unsalted (sweet) butter, melted	*100 g*	*4 oz*	*½ cup*

1 Boil the potatoes until tender, then drain and mash until fluffy. Keep them warm.

2 Meanwhile, boil the spring onions in the milk for 5 minutes.

3 Beat the spring onions and milk into the mashed potatoes and season to taste with salt and pepper.

4 Spoon the mixture into individual bowls and make a well in the centre of each one. Fill the wells with the melted butter and serve at once.

🕐 **Preparation and cooking time:** 20 minutes

Colcannon

Colcannon is similar to Champ (page 76), but is made with cabbage or kale.

Serves 4

	METRIC	IMPERIAL	AMERICAN
Potatoes, peeled and quartered	450 g	1 lb	1 lb
Cabbage, thinly shredded	450 g	1 lb	1 lb
Leek, chopped	1	1	1
Milk or single (light) cream	150 ml	¼ pt	⅔ cup
A pinch of ground mace			
Salt and freshly ground black pepper			
Unsalted (sweet) butter, melted	100 g	4 oz	½ cup

1 Cook the potatoes and cabbage separately in boiling water until tender, then drain well.

2 Meanwhile, boil the leek in the milk or cream for about 5 minutes.

3 Mash the potatoes until fluffy, then stir in the cabbage. Beat in the milk or cream and leek and season to taste with mace, salt and pepper.

4 Spoon into individual bowls and make a well in the centre of each one. Fill the wells with the melted butter and serve at once.

⏱ **Preparation and cooking time:** 20 minutes

Cabbage with Bacon

SERVES 4

	METRIC	IMPERIAL	AMERICAN
Savoy cabbage, halved and tough stem removed	1	1	1
Lean bacon rashers (slices), rinded	225 g	8 oz	8 oz
Allspice berries	4	4	4
Salt and freshly ground black pepper			
Bacon or chicken stock	300 ml	½ pt	1¼ cups

1 Cook the cabbage in boiling salted water for about 15 minutes, then drain well and chop.

2 Line the base of a casserole dish (Dutch oven) with half the bacon rashers and place the cabbage on top. Add the allspice berries and season with salt and pepper (be sparing with the salt if you are using bacon stock). Top with the remaining bacon and pour over just enough stock to cover the cabbage.

3 Cover and simmer gently for 45 minutes until the ingredients are very tender and almost all the stock has been absorbed.

🕑 **Preparation and cooking time:** 1¼ hours

Slow-cooked Celery with Bacon

SERVES 4

	METRIC	IMPERIAL	AMERICAN
Small head of celery, cut into chunks	1	1	1
Onion, sliced	1	1	2
Carrot, sliced	1	1	1
Streaky bacon rashers (slices), rinded and chopped	4	4	4
Vegetable stock	300 ml	½ pt	1¼ cups
Bouquet garni sachet	1	1	1
Salt and freshly ground black pepper			
Chopped fresh parsley	15 ml	1 tbsp	1 tbsp

1 Place all the ingredients except the parsley in a large, heavy-based saucepan.

2 Bring to the boil, then reduce the heat, cover and simmer very gently for about 50 minutes or until the celery is very tender, adding a little more stock during cooking if necessary.

3 Taste and adjust the seasoning and sprinkle with parsley before serving.

🕐 **Preparation and cooking time:** 1 hour

Kale with Cream and Nutmeg

SERVES 4

	METRIC	IMPERIAL	AMERICAN
Curly kale	450 g	1 lb	1 lb
Butter or margarine	25 g	1 oz	2 tbsp
Double (heavy) cream	30 ml	2 tbsp	2 tbsp
Vegetable stock	45 ml	3 tbsp	3 tbsp
A pinch of grated nutmeg, plus extra for sprinkling			
Salt and freshly ground black pepper			

1 Remove any tough stalks from the kale and wash it well, then place it in a large saucepan with only the water that is clinging to the leaves. Cover and cook very gently for about 10 minutes until tender. Drain off any excess water and chop finely.

2 Return the kale to the saucepan with the butter or margarine, cream, stock and a pinch of nutmeg, seasoning to taste with salt and pepper. Mix well over a medium heat until all the ingredients are well combined and the liquid has reduced by half.

3 Serve hot, sprinkled with a little more nutmeg.

🕐 **Preparation and cooking time:** 20 minutes

Stuffed Mushrooms

SERVES 4

	METRIC	IMPERIAL	AMERICAN
Large flat mushrooms	8	8	8
Vegetable or chicken stock	75 ml	5 tbsp	5 tbsp
Butter or margarine	50 g	2 oz	¼ cup
Onion, chopped	1	1	1
Sausagemeat	100 g	4 oz	4 oz
Fresh wholemeal breadcrumbs	75 g	3 oz	1½ cups
Chopped fresh parsley	15 ml	1 tbsp	1 tbsp
Salt and freshly ground black pepper			

1 Remove the mushroom stalks and chop them. Place the caps gill-side up in a shallow, greased, ovenproof dish and spoon over the stock.

2 Melt the butter or margarine and fry (sauté) the onion until softened but not browned. Stir in the chopped mushroom stalks and the sausagemeat and fry, stirring, until browned and well mixed.

3 Remove from the heat and stir in the breadcrumbs and parsley and season with salt and pepper.

4 Spoon the stuffing over the mushrooms and press down gently.

5 Bake in a preheated oven at 180°C/350°F/gas mark 4 for about 20 minutes until the mushrooms are tender and the stuffing is cooked through and golden on top.

⊕ **Preparation and cooking time:** 35 minutes

Baked Onions

SERVES 4

	METRIC	IMPERIAL	AMERICAN
Onions	4	4	4
Soft brown sugar	15 ml	1 tbsp	1 tbsp
Chopped fresh parsley	15 ml	1 tbsp	1 tbsp
Salt and freshly ground black pepper			
Butter or margarine	50 g	2 oz	¼ cup
Vegetable or chicken stock	600 ml	1 pt	2½ cups

1 Cut the tops and bottoms off the onions so that they stand upright. Place them in a saucepan, cover with cold water and bring to the boil. Reduce the heat, simmer for 10 minutes, then drain thoroughly.

2 Place the onions in a casserole dish (Dutch oven). Sprinkle with the sugar and parsley, season with salt and pepper and place a knob of butter or margarine on top of each one. Pour the stock around the onions.

3 Cover and cook in a preheated oven at 180°C/350°F/ gas mark 4 for 2 hours until very tender.

⏱ **Preparation and cooking time:** 2¼ hours

Sweet Parsnips

SERVES 4

	METRIC	IMPERIAL	AMERICAN
Parsnips, chopped	450 g	1 lb	1 lb
Cooking (tart) apples, peeled, cored and sliced	450 g	1 lb	1 lb
Water	45 ml	3 tbsp	3 tbsp
Butter or margarine	25 g	1 oz	2 tbsp
Ground cinnamon	2.5 ml	½ tsp	½ tsp
A pinch of ground cloves			
A pinch of grated nutmeg			
Salt and freshly ground black pepper			

1 Cook the parsnips in boiling water for about 8 minutes until tender, then drain well.

2 Meanwhile, cook the apples and water gently in a separate saucepan for about 8 minutes until soft.

3 Add the parsnips to the apples with the butter or margarine and spices and season with salt and pepper. Mash all the ingredients together until smooth. Heat through very gently before serving.

🕐 **Preparation and cooking time:** 15 minutes

Fried Parsnip Cakes

SERVES 4

	METRIC	IMPERIAL	AMERICAN
Parsnips, diced	450 g	1 lb	1 lb
Plain (all-purpose) flour	25 g	1 oz	¼ cup
Butter or margarine	25 g	1 oz	2 tbsp
A pinch of ground mace			
Salt and freshly ground black pepper			
Egg, lightly beaten	1	1	1
Fresh white breadcrumbs	50 g	2 oz	1 cup
Oil	30 ml	2 tbsp	2 tbsp

1 Cook the parsnips in boiling salted water for about 10 minutes until tender, then drain and mash.

2 Blend in half the flour with all the butter or margarine and mace, and season to taste with salt and pepper. Using floured hands, shape into flat cakes and dust with the remaining flour, shaking off any excess.

3 Dip in the beaten egg, then coat in breadcrumbs.

4 Heat the oil in a large frying-pan (skillet) and fry (sauté) the cakes for about 15 minutes until golden brown on both sides.

⏲ **Preparation and cooking time:** 30 minutes

Irish Swede Pudding

SERVES 4

	METRIC	IMPERIAL	AMERICAN
Swede (rutabaga), diced	450 g	1 lb	1 lb
Butter or margarine	50 g	2 oz	¼ cup
Fresh wholemeal breadcrumbs	45 ml	3 tbsp	3 tbsp
Milk	45 ml	3 tbsp	3 tbsp
Egg, lightly beaten	1	1	1
A pinch of ground cinnamon			
A pinch of sugar			
Salt and freshly ground black pepper			

1 Cook the swede in boiling salted water for about 10 minutes until tender, then drain and mash.

2 Mix in half the butter or margarine and all the remaining ingredients, seasoning to taste with salt and pepper. Spoon into an ovenproof dish and dot with the remaining butter or margarine.

3 Bake in a preheated oven at 180°C/350°F/gas mark 4 for about 45 minutes until golden on top.

🕐 **Preparation and cooking time:** 1 hour

Irish Turnips

SERVES 4

	METRIC	IMPERIAL	AMERICAN
Turnips	450 g	1 lb	1 lb
Butter or margarine	50 g	2 oz	¼ cup
Salt and freshly ground black pepper			
Snipped fresh chives	15 ml	1 tbsp	1 tbsp

1 Cook the turnips in boiling salted water for about 20 minutes until tender (the cooking time will vary, depending on the size and age of the turnips). Drain and dice.

2 Melt the butter or margarine in a heavy-based frying pan (skillet) and fry (sauté) the turnips for 5–10 minutes until golden on all sides.

3 Season well, then spoon the turnips and the melted butter or margine into a warmed serving dish and serve sprinkled with chives.

⊙ **Preparation and cooking time:** 30 minutes

Desserts, Sweets and Drinks

I rish desserts, like so many of the recipes in this book, make the most of fresh produce. Hedgerow fruits, such as blackberries, are readily available and apples, gooseberries and rhubarb all grow well in the cool, temperate climate and combine beautifully with oats and honey to make simple, tasty and nourishing puddings. This section contains everything from glorious, comforting hot desserts such as Steamed Oat and Honey Pudding (page 94) and Rhubarb and Apple Crumble (page 89) to the light and unusual Carageen and Lemon Pudding (page 100) and the wicked Whiskey Trifle (page 102). We've also slotted in a traditional breakfast dish, Stirabout (page 103), which makes a warming start to a winter day.

Apple Pie

SERVES 4

	METRIC	IMPERIAL	AMERICAN
Plain (all-purpose) flour	225 g	8 oz	2 cups
A pinch of salt			
Butter or margarine	50 g	2 oz	¼ cup
Lard (shortening) or			
vegetable fat	50 g	2 oz	¼ cup
Cold water	30 ml	2 tbsp	2 tbsp
Cooking (tart) apples, peeled,			
cored and thinly sliced	900 g	2 lb	2 lb
Whole cloves	2	2	2
Soft brown sugar	45 ml	3 tbsp	3 tbsp
Milk	15 ml	1 tbsp	1 tbsp
Cream or custard, to serve			

1 Mix the flour and salt in a bowl, then, using your fingertips, rub in the butter or margarine and lard or vegetable fat until the mixture resembles breadcrumbs. Add enough of the cold water to mix to a firm dough.

2 Roll out three-quarters of the pastry (paste) on a lightly floured surface and use to line a greased 20 cm/8 in pie dish. Cover with the apples, place the cloves on top and sprinkle with the sugar.

3 Roll out the remaining pastry and use to cover the pie, moistening the edges of the pastry base to seal on the lid. Flute the edges and decorate the top with trimmings, if liked. Cut a vent in the top and brush with milk.

4 Bake in a preheated oven at 200°C/400°F/gas mark 6 for about 30 minutes until the pastry is golden.

5 Serve with cream or custard.

⊘ **Preparation and cooking time:** 45 minutes

Rhubarb and Apple Crumble

You can substitute gooseberries for the rhubarb and apple, and use the same method to make Gooseberry Crumble, for a change.

SERVES 4

	METRIC	IMPERIAL	AMERICAN
Rhubarb, cut into chunks	450 g	1 lb	1 lb
Cooking (tart) apples, peeled, cored and sliced	450 g	1 lb	1 lb
Caster (superfine) sugar	175 g	6 oz	¾ cup
Self-raising (self-rising) flour	225 g	8 oz	2 cups
Butter or margarine	100 g	4 oz	½ cup
Soft brown sugar	100 g	4 oz	½ cup
Mixed (apple-pie) spice	2.5 ml	½ tsp	½ tsp
Single (light) cream, to serve			

1 Mix together the rhubarb, apples and caster sugar in an ovenproof dish.

2 Place the flour in a bowl and, using your fingertips, rub in the butter or margarine until the mixture resembles breadcrumbs. Stir in the brown sugar and mixed spice. Sprinkle over the fruit.

3 Bake in a preheated oven at 180°C/350°F/gas mark 4 for 45 minutes until the fruit is tender and the topping golden brown.

4 Serve hot with cream.

🕐 **Preparation and cooking time:** 1 hour

Steamed Apple Pudding

SERVES 4

	METRIC	IMPERIAL	AMERICAN
Cooking (tart) apples, peeled, cored and sliced	900 g	2 lb	2 lb
Lemon juice	10 ml	2 tsp	2 tsp
Caster (superfine) sugar	100 g	4 oz	½ cup
Whole cloves (optional)	2	2	2
Self-raising (self-rising) flour	175 g	6 oz	1½ cups
A pinch of salt			
Shredded (chopped) suet	75 g	3 oz	⅓ cup
Water	30 ml	2 tbsp	2 tbsp
Custard, to serve			

1 Place the apples, lemon juice, sugar and cloves, if using, in a saucepan and moisten with a little water. Bring to a simmer and cook very gently for about 15 minutes until the apples are just tender but not mushy.

2 Meanwhile, mix the flour, salt and suet, then work in enough of the water to make a soft but not sticky dough.

3 Roll out about three-quarters of the dough on a lightly floured surface and to line a greased 1.2 litre/2 pt/5 cup pudding basin.

4 Spoon the apples into the pastry (paste). Roll out the remaining dough to make a lid, moistening the edges to seal it to the base.

5 Cover with pleated greaseproof (waxed) paper and place in a saucepan. Fill the saucepan with enough water to come halfway up the sides of the basin. Bring to the boil, cover and steam for 1 hour, topping up with boiling water as necessary.

6 Turn out and serve with custard.

⊘ **Preparation and cooking time:** 1½ hours

Baked Apple Pastry

SERVES 4

	METRIC	IMPERIAL	AMERICAN
Soft brown sugar	50 g	2 oz	¼ cup
Raisins	50 g	2 oz	⅓ cup
Ground cinnamon	2.5 ml	½ tsp	½ tsp
Eating (dessert) apples, peeled and cored	4	4	4
Puff pastry (paste)	350 g	12 oz	12 oz
Egg, beaten	1	1	1
Double (heavy) cream, whipped	300 ml	½ pt	1¼ cups

1 Mix together the sugar, raisins and cinnamon and stuff into the centres of the apples.

2 Roll out the pastry on a lightly floured surface and cut out four 20 cm/8 in rounds. Brush the edges with egg.

3 Place an apple in the centre of each round and draw up the pastry, sealing it at the top. Brush with the remaining egg.

4 Bake in a preheated oven at 200°C/400°F/gas mark 6 for 40 minutes until the pastry is cooked and the apples soft.

5 Serve with whipped cream.

🕐 **Preparation and cooking time:** 50 minutes

Apple Fritters

SERVES 4

	METRIC	IMPERIAL	AMERICAN
Plain (all-purpose) flour	150 g	5 oz	1¼ cups
A pinch of salt			
Eggs, separated	2	2	2
Butter or margarine, melted and cooled	15 ml	1 tbsp	1 tbsp
Water	150 ml	¼ pt	⅔ cup
Large eating (dessert) apples	2	2	2
Oil, for deep-frying			
Caster (superfine) sugar and lemon juice, to serve			

1 Place the flour and salt in a bowl and make a well in the centre. Add the egg yolks and butter or margarine. Gradually whisk in the flour until smooth. Whisk in the water to make a smooth batter. Leave to stand while you prepare the apples.

2 Peel and core the apples, then cut them into rings 5 cm/½ in thick.

3 Whisk the egg whites until stiff but not dry, then fold them into the batter.

4 Dip the apple slices into the batter, then deep-fry in hot oil for about 4 minutes until golden, turning once. Depending on the size of your pan, you may have to do this in batches.

5 Drain on kitchen paper (paper towels) and serve sprinkled with sugar and lemon juice.

⊘ **Preparation and cooking time:** 30 minutes

Apple and Barley Pudding

SERVES 4

	METRIC	IMPERIAL	AMERICAN
Pearl barley	60 ml	4 tbsp	4 tbsp
Water	1 litre	1¾ pts	4¼ cups
Eating (dessert) apples, peeled, cored and sliced	700 g	1½ lb	1½ lb
Caster (superfine) sugar	50 g	2 oz	¼ cup
Lemon juice	15 ml	1 tbsp	1 tbsp
Double (heavy) cream, lightly whipped	150 ml	¼ pt	⅔ cup

1 Put the barley and water in a saucepan and bring to the boil. Reduce the heat and simmer for 20 minutes until the barley is beginning to soften.

2 Add the apples and continue to simmer gently for about 10 minutes, stirring occasionally, until the barley and apples are both tender.

3 Purée in a food processor or blender or rub through a sieve (strainer), then return to the saucepan. Add the sugar and lemon juice and bring to the boil again, stirring to mix all the ingredients.

4 Spoon into a serving bowl, leave to cool, then chill.

5 Stir in the cream before serving.

🕐 **Preparation and cooking time:** 30 minutes plus chilling

93

Steamed Oat and Honey Pudding

SERVES 4

	METRIC	IMPERIAL	AMERICAN
Milk	450 ml	¾ pt	2 cups
Rolled oats	175 g	6 oz	1½ cups
Caster (superfine) sugar	50 g	2 oz	¼ cup
Clear honey	15 ml	1 tbsp	1 tbsp
Butter or margarine	25 g	1 oz	2 tbsp
Finely grated rind of 1 lemon			
Ground cinnamon	2.5 ml	½ tsp	½ tsp
Eggs, separated	3	3	3
Clear honey and single (light) cream, to serve			

1 Pour the milk into a saucepan and bring to the boil. Sprinkle on the oats and stir over a low heat for 5 minutes.

2 Stir in the sugar, honey, butter or margarine, lemon rind and cinnamon. Remove from the heat.

3 Beat in the egg yolks.

4 Beat the egg whites until stiff, then fold them into the mixture.

5 Spoon the mixture into a greased 1.2 litre/2 pt/5 cup pudding basin and cover with pleated greaseproof (waxed) paper. Place in a saucepan and surround with enough boiling water to come halfway up the sides of the basin. Cover and simmer for 2–2½ hours until set, topping up the boiling water as necessary.

6 Turn out on to a serving dish and serve hot with honey and cream.

⏰ **Preparation and cooking time:** 2¼–2¾ hours

Irish Bread Pudding

*This is a great way to use up almost any kind of leftover bread
– an ordinary brown or white loaf and fruited and potato breads all
work well.*

SERVES 4

	METRIC	IMPERIAL	AMERICAN
Eggs	5	5	5
Milk	250 ml	8 fl oz	1 cup
Single (light) cream	120 ml	4 fl oz	½ cup
Ground cinnamon	2.5 ml	½ tsp	½ tsp
Grated nutmeg	2.5 ml	½ tsp	½ tsp
Vanilla essence (extract)	5 ml	1 tsp	1 tsp
Stale bread of any kind, torn into pieces	450 g	1 lb	1 lb
Butter or margarine	50 g	2 oz	¼ cup
Soft brown sugar	100 g	4 oz	½ cup
Chopped mixed nuts	50 g	2 oz	½ cup
Rolled oats	50 g	2 oz	½ cup
Whipped cream, to serve			

1 Whisk together the eggs, milk, cream, spices and vanilla essence in an ovenproof dish.

2 Add the bread and press it down so that it absorbs the mixture. Leave to soak for at least 2 hours.

3 Blend together the butter or margarine and sugar, then work in the nuts and oats. Spoon over the top of the bread mixture.

4 Bake in a preheated oven at 180°C/350°F/gas mark 4 for 40 minutes until springy to the touch and golden brown on top.

5 Serve hot with whipped cream or leave until cold, then cut into slices.

⊘ **Preparation and cooking time:** 50 minutes plus soaking

Blackcap Pudding

SERVES 4

	METRIC	IMPERIAL	AMERICAN
Blackcurrants	225 g	8 oz	8 oz
Grated rind and juice of ½ lemon			
Caster (superfine) sugar	50 g	2 oz	¼ cup
Plain (all-purpose) flour	100 g	4 oz	1 cup
Baking powder	2.5 ml	½ tsp	½ tsp
Fresh white breadcrumbs	100 g	4 oz	2 cups
Eggs, lightly beaten	2	2	2
Milk	300 ml	½ pt	1¼ cups
Whipped cream or custard, to serve			

1 Rinse the blackcurrants and place in a saucepan with only the water that is clinging to them. Add the lemon rind and juice and half the sugar and simmer gently for 6 minutes, then spoon into a greased 1.2 litre/2 pt/5 cup pudding basin.

2 Mix the remaining sugar with the flour, baking powder and breadcrumbs. Beat in the eggs and milk, then leave to stand for 15 minutes. Spoon over the blackcurrants, then cover with pleated greaseproof (waxed) paper and foil.

3 Place the basin in a large saucepan and pour in enough boiling water to come halfway up the sides of the basin. Cover and steam for 2–2½ hours until set, topping up the boiling water as necessary.

4 Carefully loosen the edges of the pudding, then turn it out on to a serving plate and serve with whipped cream or custard.

⏲ **Preparation and cooking time:** 2¼–2¾ hours plus standing

Blackberry Sorbet

You can make this refreshing sorbet with hedgerow blackberries or any similar fruits.

SERVES 4

	METRIC	IMPERIAL	AMERICAN
Blackberries	*450 g*	*1 lb*	*1 lb*
Caster (superfine) sugar	*100 g*	*4 oz*	*½ cup*
Water	*120 ml*	*4 fl oz*	*½ cup*
Egg whites	*2*	*2*	*2*

1 Purée the blackberries in a blender or food processor, then rub through a sieve (strainer) to remove the pips.

2 Dissolve the sugar in the water over a low heat, then boil for about 5 minutes to make a thick syrup. Add the blackberry purée and simmer for a further 2 minutes. Leave to cool.

3 Beat the egg whites until stiff, then fold them into the blackberries. Spoon into a freezer container and freeze for 1 hour.

4 Remove from the freezer and stir to break up the ice crystals, then return to the freezer. Repeat the stirring every hour or so for the next 4 hours.

5 Remove from the freezer 30 minutes before serving to soften.

🕐 **Preparation and cooking time:** 15 minutes plus freezing and softening

Gooseberry Fool

Sharp fruits are best for this dessert so, for a change, rhubarb makes a good substitute for the gooseberries.

SERVES 4

	METRIC	IMPERIAL	AMERICAN
Gooseberries	450 g	1 lb	1 lb
Water	300 ml	½ pt	1¼ cups
Clear honey	30 ml	2 tbsp	2 tbsp
Caster (superfine) sugar	60 ml	4 tbsp	4 tbsp
Powdered gelatine	20 ml	4 tsp	4 tsp
Double (heavy) cream	150 ml	¼ pt	⅔ cup

1 Place the gooseberries and water in a saucepan, bring to the boil, then reduce the heat, partially cover and simmer for about 20 minutes until the fruit is soft. Purée in a blender or food processor, then rub through a sieve (strainer) to remove the seeds.

2 Return the purée to the pan, add the honey and sugar and bring to the boil.

3 Meanwhile, sprinkle the gelatine over 60 ml/4 tbsp of water in a small bowl. Stand the bowl in a pan of hot water until the gelatine dissolves. Stir into the gooseberry purée and until leave cool and beginning to set.

4 Whip the cream until stiff, then fold it into the purée. Spoon into individual glasses and chill before serving.

🕐 **Preparation and cooking time:** 30 minutes plus setting and chilling

Donegal Oat Cream

SERVES 4

	METRIC	IMPERIAL	AMERICAN
Medium oatmeal	100 g	4 oz	1 cup
Milk	450 ml	¾ pt	2 cups
Powdered gelatine	15 g	½ oz	1 tbsp
Orange juice	15 ml	1 tbsp	1 tbsp
Water	30 ml	2 tbsp	2 tbsp
Egg, separated	1	1	1
Soft brown sugar	30 ml	2 tbsp	2 tbsp
Grated nutmeg	2.5 ml	½ tsp	½ tsp
Grated rind and juice of 1 lemon			
Double (heavy) cream	250 ml	8 fl oz	1 cup
Fruit purée or clear honey, to serve			

1 Soak the oatmeal in the milk for 30 minutes.

2 Transfer to a saucepan and bring to the boil, then reduce the heat and simmer gently for 4 minutes, stirring. Remove from the heat and leave to cool slightly.

3 Put the gelatine, orange juice and water in a small bowl and place in a pan of hot water to dissolve the gelatine. Stir into the warm oatmeal mixture until thoroughly mixed.

4 Whisk the egg yolk and sugar together well, then stir into the oatmeal with the nutmeg and lemon rind and juice. Whisk the egg white until firm, then fold into the mixture.

5 Whip the cream until stiff, then fold into the mixture.

6 Chill, then serve topped with fruit purée of your choice or with a drizzle of honey.

🕐 **Preparation and cooking time:** 40 minutes plus chilling

Carageen and Lemon Pudding

Carageen is a seaweed, also known as Irish moss or sea moss. It is available in delicatessens or health food shops.

SERVES 4

	METRIC	IMPERIAL	AMERICAN
Dried carageen	30 g	1½ oz	1½ oz
Juice and grated rind of 1 lemon			
Clear honey	15 ml	1 tbsp	1 tbsp
Water	600 ml	1 pt	2½ cups
Double (heavy) cream	150 ml	¼ pt	⅔ cup
Egg white	1	1	1
Lemon, sliced	1	1	1

1 Place the carageen in a small bowl and cover with boiling water. Leave to soak for 30 minutes, then drain.

2 Place the carageen in a saucepan with the lemon juice and rind, honey and water, bring to the boil, then reduce the heat and simmer for 30 minutes, stirring occasionally.

3 Place a fine sieve (strainer) over a bowl, pour in the mixture and leave to strain and cool.

4 Whisk the cream until thick, then fold into the cooled mixture.

5 Whisk the egg white until stiff, then fold into the mixture. Spoon into a 1.2 litre/2 pt/5 cup pudding basin and chill until set.

6 Turn out and serve garnished with lemon slices.

⏱ **Preparation and cooking time:** 40 minutes plus soaking, chilling and setting

Carageen Jelly

SERVES 4

	METRIC	IMPERIAL	AMERICAN
Carageen	25 g	1 oz	1 oz
Milk	600 ml	1 pt	2½ cups
Caster (superfine) sugar	30 ml	2 tbsp	2 tbsp
A pinch of salt			
Rhubarb, cut into chunks	225 g	8 oz	8 oz

1 Soak the carageen in water for about 20 minutes, then drain and squeeze out any excess water.

2 Place in a saucepan with the milk, half the sugar and the salt, bring to a simmer, then cook gently for 30 minutes.

3 Meanwhile, rinse the rhubarb and place in a saucepan with the remaining sugar and the water that is clinging to the stems. Bring to a simmer, then cook gently for about 10 minutes until soft.

4 Strain the carageen milk into a glass serving bowl, then stir in the rhubarb. Leave to set before serving.

⏱ **Preparation and cooking time:** 45 minutes plus setting

Whiskey Trifle

SERVES 4

	METRIC	IMPERIAL	AMERICAN
Stale 20 cm/8 in sponge cake, *chopped*	1	1	1
Sweet sherry	150 ml	¼ pt	⅔ cup
Irish whiskey	45 ml	3 tbsp	3 tbsp
Raspberry jam (conserve)	60 ml	4 tbsp	4 tbsp
Thick custard	300 ml	½ pt	1¼ cups
Double (heavy) cream	300 ml	½ pt	1¼ cups

1 Place the cake pieces in the base of a serving bowl, pour over the sherry and whiskey and leave to soak in.

2 Stir in the jam and pour the custard over the top.

3 Whip the cream until stiff and spread over the custard. Chill before serving.

🕐 **Preparation time:** 5 minutes plus soaking and chilling

Yellow Man

This sticky toffee is a delicious Irish treat.

SERVES 4

	METRIC	IMPERIAL	AMERICAN
Golden (light corn) syrup	450 g	1 lb	1½ cups
Soft brown sugar	225 g	8 oz	1 cup
Butter or margarine	25 g	1 oz	2 tbsp
Distilled malt vinegar	30 ml	2 tbsp	2 tbsp
Bicarbonate of soda *(baking soda)*	5 ml	1 tsp	1 tsp

1 Place all the ingredients except the bicarbonate of soda in a large, heavy-based saucepan and heat gently until the sugar and butter or margarine have melted.

2 Bring to a rapid boil and boil until the syrup has reached 155°C/298°F. (If you do not have a sugar thermometer, place a drop of the mixture in a glass of cold water, then pick it up between your finger and thumb: the thread should snap when you separate your fingers.)

3 Stir in the bicarbonate of soda; the mixture will foam. Pour on to a greased work surface and leave until cool enough to handle, then, with greased hands, fold the mixture from the edges to the centre and pull. Repeat until it turns yellow.

4 Allow to cool and harden, then break into chunks using a toffee hammer.

🕐 **Preparation and cooking time:** 45 minutes

Stirabout

This is the perfect, healthy breakfast, so it doesn't really fit into any of the book's categories – however, it is such a traditional Irish dish that I didn't want to leave it out. You can use rolled oats instead of oatmeal; they do not need to be soaked, but you will need to add more liquid when cooking and simmer the porridge for a little longer.

SERVES 2

	METRIC	IMPERIAL	AMERICAN
Medium oatmeal	100 g	4 oz	1 cup
Water	600 ml	1 pt	2½ cups
A pinch of salt			
Clear honey	15 ml	1 tbsp	1 tbsp
Milk or single (light) cream	15 ml	1 tsp	1 tbsp

1 Soak the oatmeal in the water overnight.

2 Bring to the boil, reduce the heat, then simmer gently for 10 minutes until creamy, stirring regularly.

3 Stir in the honey and milk or cream before serving.

🕐 **Preparation and cooking time:** 10 minutes plus soaking

Irish Coffee

SERVES 2

	METRIC	IMPERIAL	AMERICAN
Hot coffee	450 ml	¾ pt	2 cups
Soft brown sugar	10 ml	2 tsp	2 tsp
Irish whiskey	60 ml	4 tbsp	4 tbsp
Double (heavy) cream	60 ml	4 tbsp	4 tbsp

1 Warm two Irish coffee glasses by filling them with hot water and emptying them, then filling them with almost boiling water and emptying them again.

2 Pour the coffee into the glasses, add the sugar and stir to dissolve, then add the whiskey.

3 Hold a spoon bowl-side up over the top of the coffee and pour the cream on to the back of the spoon so it flows on to the top of the coffee, forming a thick layer. Serve at once.

⊘ **Preparation and cooking time:** 5 minutes

Hot Whiskey

SERVES 2

	METRIC	IMPERIAL	AMERICAN
Irish whiskey	120 ml	4 fl oz	½ cup
Lemon slices	2	2	2
Whole cloves	2	2	2
Caster (superfine) sugar	5–10 ml	1–2 tsp	1–2 tsp

1 Warm two whiskey glasses by filling them with hot water and emptying them, then filling them with almost boiling water and emptying them again.

2 Place the whiskey, lemon and cloves in the glasses, then half-fill with boiling water and stir in the sugar to taste. Serve at once.

⊘ **Preparation and cooking time:** 5 minutes

Bread, Cakes and Biscuits

n this chapter you will find a great variety of interesting fruit breads and griddle-baked breads and cakes, plus several different kinds of that best-known of Irish bread recipes, soda bread. Soda breads are delicious and very simple to make, but must be eaten fresh.

Soda Bread

If you don't have the traditional buttermilk, you can use fresh milk and add 5 ml/1 tsp cream of tartar.

MAKES ONE 900 G/2 LB LOAF

	METRIC	IMPERIAL	AMERICAN
Plain (all-purpose) flour	900 g	2 lb	8 cups
Bicarbonate of soda			
(baking soda)	5 ml	1 tsp	1 tsp
Salt	5 ml	1 tsp	1 tsp
Buttermilk	600 ml	1 pt	2½ cups

1 Mix together the flour, bicarbonate of soda and salt and make a well in the centre.

2 Gradually add just enough buttermilk to mix to a soft but not sticky dough and knead lightly until smooth.

3 Shape into a 23 cm/9 in round, place on a greased baking (cookie) sheet and cut a deep cross in the top.

4 Bake in a preheated oven at 200°C/400°F/gas mark 6 for about 1 hour until risen and golden and the bread sounds hollow when tapped on the base.

⏱ **Preparation and cooking time:** 1¼ hours

Soda Farls

Make up the soda bread dough and cut it into quarters. Cook on a greased griddle or heavy-based frying pan (skillet) for about 15 minutes each side until cooked through and golden.

Fruit Soda Bread

Add 175 g/6 oz/1 cup raisins or sultanas (golden raisins) and 15 ml/1 tbsp soft brown sugar to the soda bread dough.

Wholemeal Soda Bread

MAKES ONE 900 G/2 LB LOAF

	METRIC	IMPERIAL	AMERICAN
Plain wholemeal flour	450 g	1 lb	4 cups
Plain (all-purpose) flour	350 g	12 oz	3 cups
Rolled oats	50 g	2 oz	½ cup
Caster (superfine) sugar	10 ml	2 tsp	2 tsp
Bicarbonate of soda (baking soda)	10 ml	2 tsp	2 tsp
A pinch of salt			
Buttermilk	600 ml	1 pt	2½ cups

1 Mix together the flours, oats, sugar, bicarbonate of soda and salt and make a well in the centre.

2 Gradually add just enough buttermilk to mix to a soft but not sticky dough and knead lightly until just smooth.

3 Shape into a 23 cm/9 in round, place on a greased baking (cookie) sheet and cut a deep cross in the top.

4 Bake in a preheated oven at 200°C/400°F/gas mark 6 for about 1 hour until risen and golden and the bread sounds hollow when tapped on the base.

🕐 **Preparation and cooking time:** 1¼ hours

Apple Soda Bread

MAKES ONE 900 G/2 LB LOAF

	METRIC	IMPERIAL	AMERICAN
Cooking (tart) apples, peeled,			
cored and chopped	*450 g*	*1 lb*	*1 lb*
Soft brown sugar	*25 g*	*1 oz*	*2 tbsp*
1 quantity of soda bread			
dough (page 106)			

1 Cook the apples with the sugar and 15 ml/1 tbsp water for about 10 minutes until soft.

2 Halve the dough and roll out on a lightly floured surface to make two rounds about 1 cm/½ in thick.

3 Place one round on a greased baking (cookie) sheet and moisten the edges with water. Spoon the apples into the centre and top with the other round of dough, sealing the edges together.

4 Bake in a preheated oven at 180°C/350°F/gas mark 4 for 35–40 minutes until light golden brown. Alternatively, cook on a greased griddle or in a heavy-based frying pan (skillet) for 10–15 minutes each side.

🕐 **Preparation and cooking time:** 40–45 minutes

Potato Farls

The Irish love to serve this potato bread with their hearty breakfasts.
'Farl' actually means 'quarter', although you can cut the dough into
rounds if you prefer. You can also add some fresh herbs to the dough
as a variation.

SERVES 4

	METRIC	IMPERIAL	AMERICAN
Plain (all-purpose) flour	*75 g*	*3 oz*	*¾ cup*
Baking powder	*2.5 ml*	*½ tsp*	*½ tsp*
A pinch of salt			
Butter or margarine	*25 g*	*1 oz*	*2 tbsp*
Mashed potatoes	*225 g*	*8 oz*	*8 oz*
Milk	*30 ml*	*2 tbsp*	*2 tbsp*
Butter, to serve			

1 Mix together the flour, baking powder and salt in a
bowl, then, using your fingertips, rub in the butter or
margarine until the mixture resembles breadcrumbs.

2 Stir in the mashed potatoes and enough of the milk to
make a soft but not loose dough.

3 Roll out on a lightly floured surface to a round about
1 cm/½ in thick and mark into quarters, without cutting
right through the base.

4 Place on a greased baking (cookie) sheet and bake in a
preheated oven at 200°C/400°F/gas mark 6 for about
20 minutes until golden. Alternatively, place on a greased
griddle and cook for about 10 minutes over a medium heat.

5 Serve with plenty of butter.

⏲ **Preparation and cooking time:** 30 minutes

Oatmeal and Wheatgerm Bread

MAKES ONE 450 G/1 LB LOAF

	METRIC	IMPERIAL	AMERICAN
Wholemeal flour	225 g	8 oz	2 cups
Strong plain (bread) flour	100 g	4 oz	1 cup
Wheatgerm	50 g	2 oz	½ cup
Medium oatmeal	50 g	2 oz	½ cup
Bicarbonate of soda (baking soda)	15 ml	1 tbsp	1 tbsp
Egg, lightly beaten	1	1	1
Buttermilk	600 ml	1 pt	2½ cups
Butter or margarine, to serve			

1 Mix together the flours, wheatgerm, oatmeal and bicarbonate of soda and make a well in the centre. Gradually work in the egg and enough of the buttermilk to make a soft but not sticky dough.

2 Shape into a 20 cm/8 in round, place on a greased baking (cookie) sheet and cut a cross in the centre.

3 Bake in a preheated oven at 200°C/400°F/gas mark 6 for 20 minutes. Reduce the oven temperature to 180°C/350°F/gas mark 4 and bake for a further 15–20 minutes until risen and golden and the loaf sounds hollow when tapped on the base.

4 Leave to cool, then serve sliced and buttered.

⊙ **Preparation and cooking time:** 40–45 minutes

Caraway Seed Loaf

MAKES ONE 900 G/2 LB LOAF

	METRIC	IMPERIAL	AMERICAN
Plain (all-purpose) flour	450 g	1 lb	4 cups
Baking powder	10 ml	2 tsp	2 tsp
A pinch of salt			
Butter or margarine	175 g	6 oz	¾ cup
Soft brown sugar	175 g	6 oz	¾ cup
Chopped mixed (candied) peel	75 g	3 oz	½ cup
Caraway seeds	10 ml	2 tsp	2 tsp
Eggs, lightly beaten	2	2	2
Milk	15–30 ml	1–2 tbsp	1–2 tbsp

1 Mix the flour, baking powder and salt in a bowl. Using your fingertips, rub in the butter or margarine, then stir in the sugar, mixed peel and half the caraway seeds. Make a well in the centre.

2 Add the eggs and enough milk to make a soft but not sticky dough.

3 Shape into a greased and lined 900 g/2 lb loaf tin (pan), brush the top with a little milk and sprinkle with the remaining caraway seeds.

4 Bake in a preheated oven at 180°C/350°F/gas mark 4 for about 1½ hours until a skewer inserted in the centre comes out clean.

⊘ **Preparation and cooking time:** 1¾ hours

Barm Brack

MAKES ONE 900 G/2 LB LOAF

	METRIC	IMPERIAL	AMERICAN
Strong plain (bread) flour	450 g	1 lb	4 cups
Butter or margarine	25 g	1 oz	2 tbsp
Caster (superfine) sugar	50 g	2 oz	¼ cup
Easy-blend dried yeast	7.5 ml	1½ tsp	1½ tsp
Ground ginger	2.5 ml	½ tsp	½ tsp
Freshly grated nutmeg	1.5 ml	¼ tsp	¼ tsp
Sultanas (golden raisins)	175 g	6 oz	1 cup
Currants	175 g	6 oz	1 cup
Chopped mixed (candied) peel	50g	2 oz	¼ cup
Warm water	300 ml	½ pt	1¼ cups

1 Place the flour in a large bowl and, using your fingertips, rub in the butter or margarine until the mixture resembles breadcrumbs.

2 Stir in 5 ml/1 tsp of the sugar, the yeast, ginger and nutmeg until well mixed. Stir in the sultanas, currants and mixed peel and make a well in the centre.

3 Gradually work in enough of the warm water to make a soft but not sticky dough and knead well until the dough leaves the sides of the bowl clean.

4 Knead on a lightly floured surface for about 10 minutes until smooth and elastic.

5 Place in an oiled bowl, cover with oiled clingfilm (plastic wrap) and leave to rise in a warm place for 1 hour until doubled in size.

6 Knead again, then shape into a large round and place on a greased baking (cookie) sheet. Cover and leave in a warm place for about 30 minutes until doubled in size.

7 Shape into a greased and lined 900 g/2 lb loaf tin (pan) and bake in a preheated oven at 230°C/450°F/gas mark 8 for 15 minutes, then reduce the oven temperature to 200°C/400°F/gas mark 6 for a further 20 minutes until risen and golden and the loaf sounds hollow when tapped on the base.

8 Dissolve the remaining sugar in 15 ml/1 tbsp hot water, then brush the syrup over the loaf and return to the oven for 2 minutes to glaze.

9 Leave to cool, then serve sliced and buttered.

⏲ **Preparation and cooking time:** 1 hour plus rising

Hot Tea Brack

MAKES TWO 450 G/1 LB LOAVES

	METRIC	IMPERIAL	AMERICAN
Raisins	*225 g*	*8 oz*	*1⅓ cups*
Sultanas (golden raisins)	*225 g*	*8 oz*	*1⅓ cups*
Currants	*175 g*	*6 oz*	*1 cup*
Hot tea	*300 ml*	*½ pt*	*1¼ cups*
Plain (all-purpose) flour	*450 g*	*1 lb*	*4 cups*
Soft brown sugar	*225 g*	*8 oz*	*1 cup*
Baking powder	*5 ml*	*1 tsp*	*1 tsp*
Mixed (apple-pie) spice	*5 ml*	*1 tsp*	*1 tsp*
Egg, lightly beaten	*1*	*1*	*1*
A little milk, to glaze			

1 Place the fruit in a bowl and pour over the hot tea. Leave to soak overnight.

2 Mix in the flour, sugar, baking powder, spice and egg until all the ingredients are well blended.

3 Spoon the mixture into two greased 450 g/1 lb loaf tins (pans) and brush the tops with milk.

4 Bake in a preheated oven at 180°C/350°F/gas mark 4 for 1¼ hours until golden on top and springy to the touch.

⏲ **Preparation and cooking time:** 1½ hours plus soaking

Porter Cake

Porter is less strong than stout, so if you replace it with Guinness or Murphy's in this recipe, use half stout and half water.

MAKES ONE 23 CM/9 IN CAKE

	METRIC	IMPERIAL	AMERICAN
Currants	225 g	8 oz	1⅓ cups
Raisins	350 g	12 oz	2 cups
Sultanas (golden raisins)	350 g	12 oz	2 cups
Porter	250 ml	8 fl oz	1 cup
Butter or margarine	225 g	8 oz	1 cup
Soft brown sugar	225 g	8 oz	1 cup
Plain (all-purpose) flour	450 g	1 lb	4 cups
Chopped mixed (candied) peel	50 g	2 oz	¼ cup
Mixed (apple-pie) spice	5 ml	1 tsp	1 tsp
Grated rind of 1 lemon			
Eggs	3	3	3
Bicarbonate of soda (baking soda)	5 ml	1 tsp	1 tsp

1 Mix the currants, raisins and sultanas with the porter and leave to soak until plump.

2 Cream together the butter or margarine and sugar until light and fluffy.

3 Mix the flour, mixed peel, spice and lemon rind. Gradually add them into the butter mixture alternately with the eggs, stirring well after each addition.

4 Pour off a little of the porter from the fruit and warm it slightly. Stir in the bicarbonate of soda, then pour over the fruit. Stir, then mix the fruit into the remaining ingredients. Spoon into a greased and lined 23 cm/9 in cake tin (pan).

5 Bake in a preheated oven at 180°C/350°F/gas mark 4 for about 1½ hours until a skewer inserted in the centre comes out clean. Cover with greaseproof (waxed) paper for the last 30 minutes if the top is overbrowning.

⏲ **Preparation and cooking time:** 1¾ hours

Boiled Fruit Cake

MAKES ONE 20 CM/8 IN CAKE

	METRIC	IMPERIAL	AMERICAN
Dried mixed fruit (fruit cake mix)	450 g	1 lb	2⅔ cups
Butter or margarine	225 g	8 oz	1 cup
Caster (superfine) sugar	350 g	12 oz	1½ cups
Eggs, lightly beaten	3	3	3
Plain (all-purpose) flour	350 g	12 oz	3 cups
Baking powder	5 ml	1 tsp	1 tsp
Mixed (apple-pie) spice	10 ml	2 tsp	2 tsp
A pinch of salt			
Chopped mixed (candied) peel	100 g	4 oz	⅔ cup
Glacé (candied) cherries, chopped	100 g	4 oz	½ cup

1 Put the dried fruit in a saucepan with just enough cold water to cover. Bring to the boil, then reduce the heat and simmer gently for 10 minutes until the fruit is soft and swollen. Leave to cool in the water for a few minutes, then drain well.

2 Cream together the butter or margarine and sugar, then gradually beat in the eggs. Fold in the flour, baking powder, mixed spice and salt.

3 Stir in the fruit, mixed peel and glacé cherries.

4 Spoon the mixture into a greased and lined 20 cm/8 in cake tin (pan) and bake in a preheated oven at 160°C/325°F/gas mark 3 for 1 hour, then reduce the oven temperature to 150°C/300°F/gas mark 2 for a further 1¼ hours until a skewer inserted in the centre comes out clean. Cover the top with a sheet of greaseproof (waxed) paper towards the end of cooking time if it is overbrowning.

🕐 **Preparation and cooking time:** 2½ hours

Whiskey Cake

MAKES ONE 20 CM/8 IN CAKE

	METRIC	IMPERIAL	AMERICAN
Raisins	225 g	8 oz	1⅓ cups
Grated rind and juice of 1 lemon			
Irish whiskey	150 ml	¼ pt	⅔ cup
Butter or margarine	175 g	6 oz	¾ cup
Soft brown sugar	175 g	6 oz	¾ cup
Plain (all-purpose) flour	175 g	6 oz	1½ cups
Baking powder	5 ml	1 tsp	1 tsp
Ground cloves	2.5 ml	½ tsp	½ tsp
A pinch of salt			
Eggs, separated	3	3	3
Icing (confectioners') sugar	225 g	8 oz	1⅓ cups
A little warm water			

1 Soak the raisins and lemon rind in the whiskey overnight.

2 Cream together the butter or margarine and sugar until light and fluffy. Mix together the flour, baking powder, cloves and salt.

3 Gradually beat the egg yolks into the butter and sugar mixture, alternating with the dry ingredients. Stir in the raisin and whiskey mixture.

4 Whisk the egg whites until stiff, then fold them into the mixture.

5 Spoon into a greased and lined 20 cm/8 in cake tin (pan) and bake in a preheated oven at 180°C/350°F/gas mark 4 for about 1½ hours until well risen and springy to the touch. Turn out on to a wire rack and leave to cool.

6 Sift the icing sugar into a bowl and make a well in the centre. Pour in half the lemon juice and gradually work in the icing sugar, adding more lemon juice and a little water until thick and smooth.

7 Transfer the cake to a plate, then slowly spoon over the icing (frosting), letting it dribble down the sides. Scoop up any pools of icing on the plate and spoon back over the cake.

⏱ **Preparation and cooking time:** 1¾ hours plus soaking

Buttermilk Bannock

MAKES ONE 20 CM/8 IN BANNOCK

	METRIC	IMPERIAL	AMERICAN
Strong plain (bread) flour	450 g	1 lb	4 cups
Baking powder	15 ml	1 tbsp	1 tbsp
Bicarbonate of soda (baking soda)	2.5 ml	½ tsp	½ tsp
A pinch of salt			
Raisins	175 g	6 oz	1 cup
Eggs	2	2	2
Buttermilk	375 ml	13 fl oz	1½ cups
Butter or margarine, to serve			

1 Mix together the flour, baking powder, bicarbonate of soda, salt and raisins and make a well in the centre.

2 Whisk the eggs with the buttermilk, then gradually work the mixture into the dry ingredients until you have a soft, slightly sticky dough.

3 Shape the dough into greased a 20 cm/8 in cake tin (pan) and cut a cross in the top. Bake in a preheated oven at 180°C/350°F/gas mark 4 for 1¼ hours until golden and cooked through.

4 Leave to cool in the tin for 30 minutes, then turn out on to a wire rack to finish cooling.

5 Serve sliced and spread with butter or margarine.

⏱ **Preparation and cooking time:** 1½ hours

Irish Coffee Cake

MAKES ONE 20 CM/8 IN CAKE

	METRIC	IMPERIAL	AMERICAN
Butter or margarine	100 g	4 oz	½ cup
Caster (superfine) sugar	100 g	4 oz	½ cup
Eggs, lightly beaten	2	2	2
Self-raising (self-rising) flour	100 g	4 oz	1 cup
Coffee essence (extract)	30 ml	2 tbsp	2 tbsp
For the coffee syrup:			
Strong black coffee	150 ml	¼ pt	⅔ cup
Soft brown sugar	100 g	4 oz	½ cup
Irish whiskey	60 ml	4 tbsp	4 tbsp
Double (heavy) or whipping cream	150 ml	¼ pt	⅔ cup
Icing (confectioners') sugar, sifted	30 ml	2 tbsp	2 tbsp

1 Cream together the butter or margarine and sugar until light and fluffy. Beat in the eggs, fold in the flour and stir in the coffee essence.

2 Spoon into a greased and lined 20 cm/8 in cake tin (pan) and bake in a preheated oven at 180°C/350°F/gas mark 4 for 35–40 minutes until golden and springy to the touch. Turn out on to a wire rack, remove the lining paper and leave to cool while you make the coffee syrup.

3 Bring the coffee to the boil with the sugar and stir until dissolved. Continue to boil for about 1 minute until the mixture thickens to a syrup. Stir in the whiskey.

4 Place the cake back in the cake tin, then spoon over the whiskey syrup and leave it to soak in.

5 Remove the cake from the tin and slice in half horizontally. Whip the cream until stiff, then sandwich the two halves together with the cream and serve sprinkled with icing sugar.

⏱ **Preparation and cooking time:** 1 hour

Ginger Cake

MAKES 9 SQUARES

	METRIC	IMPERIAL	AMERICAN
Plain (all-purpose) flour	275 g	10 oz	2½ cups
Ground cinnamon	5 ml	1 tsp	1 tsp
Ground ginger	10 ml	2 tsp	2 tsp
Bicarbonate of soda (baking soda)	5 ml	1 tsp	1 tsp
Butter or margarine	100 g	4 oz	½ cup
Golden (light corn) syrup	175 g	6 oz	½ cup
Black treacle (molasses)	175 g	6 oz	½ cup
Soft brown sugar	100 g	4 oz	½ cup
Eggs, lightly beaten	2	2	2
Hot water	150 ml	¼ pt	⅔ cup

1 Mix together the flour, spices and bicarbonate of soda in a bowl.

2 Melt the butter or margarine with the syrup, treacle and sugar, then pour the mixture into the dry ingredients. Add the eggs and water and mix well.

3 Spoon the mixture into a greased and lined 23 cm/9 in square cake tin (pan) and bake in a preheated oven at 180°C/350°F/gas mark 4 for 45 minutes until golden, well risen and springy to the touch.

4 Remove from the tin and leave on a wire rack to cool, then serve cut into squares.

🕐 **Preparation and cooking time:** 1 hour

Irish Oatcakes

MAKES ABOUT 12

	METRIC	IMPERIAL	AMERICAN
Medium oatmeal	225 g	8 oz	2 cups
Plain (all-purpose) flour	100 g	4 oz	1 cup
Salt	5 ml	1 tsp	1 tsp
Baking powder	5 ml	1 tsp	1 tsp
Water	45 ml	3 tbsp	3 tbsp
Butter or margarine	25 g	1 oz	2 tbsp
Butter, honey, jam (conserve) or cheese, to serve			

1 Mix the oatmeal, flour, salt and baking powder in a bowl and make a well in the centre.

2 Place the water in a small saucepan with the butter or margarine and bring to the boil. Pour into the dry ingredients and quickly mix to a stiff dough, adding a little more water if necessary.

3 Roll out on a lightly floured surface to about 5 mm/¼ in thick and cut into rounds with a pastry (cookie) cutter. Transfer to a greased baking (cookie) sheet and bake in a preheated oven at 180°C/350°F/gas mark 4 for about 20 minutes until golden.

4 Transfer to a wire rack to cool, then serve with butter and honey, jam or slices of cheese.

⊘ **Preparation and cooking time:** 35 minutes

Drop Scones

These are delicious, small, thick pancakes to be served spread with butter and home-made jam (conserve).

SERVES 4

	METRIC	IMPERIAL	AMERICAN
Plain (all-purpose) flour	225 g	8 oz	2 cups
Bicarbonate of soda (baking soda)	2.5 ml	½ tsp	½ tsp
Caster (superfine) sugar	5 ml	1 tsp	1 tsp
Salt	2.5 ml	½ tsp	½ tsp
Egg, lightly beaten	1	1	1
Buttermilk	300 ml	½ pt	1¼ cups
Butter or margarine and jam, to serve			

1 Mix the flour, bicarbonate of soda, sugar and salt in a large bowl and make a well in the centre.

2 Quickly beat in the egg and buttermilk just until blended; do not overbeat.

3 Cook spoonfuls of the mixture on a hot griddle or heavy-based frying pan (skillet) for a few minutes until bubbles appear on the surface, then flip them over and cook the other side until lightly browned.

4 Serve with butter or margarine and jam.

🕐 **Preparation and cooking time:** 15 minutes

Irish Butter Scones

SERVES 4

	METRIC	IMPERIAL	AMERICAN
Butter	75 g	3 oz	⅓ cup
Self-raising (self-rising) flour	225	8 oz	2 cups
A pinch of salt			
Caster (superfine) sugar	50 g	2 oz	¼ cup
Egg, lightly beaten	1	1	1
Buttermilk	45 ml	3 tbsp	3 tbsp
Butter, jam (conserve) and clotted cream, to serve			

1 Using your fingertips, rub the butter into the flour and salt until the mixture resembles breadcrumbs. Stir in the sugar. Gradually work in the egg and enough of the buttermilk to make a soft but not sticky dough.

2 Roll out the dough on a lightly floured surface to 3 cm/ 1¼ in thick and cut into rounds with a 5 cm/2 in pastry (cookie) cutter.

3 Place the scones(biscuits) on a greased baking (cookie) sheet and bake in a preheated oven at 200°C/400°F/ gas mark 6 for about 10 minutes until well risen and golden.

4 Cool, then split and spread with butter, jam and cream.

⊘ **Preparation and cooking time:** 30 minutes

Apple Scones

Add 30 ml/2 tbsp apple purée to the above mixture with the egg and buttermilk, reducing the amount of buttermilk slightly.

Fruit Scones

Add 100 g/4 oz/⅔ cup raisins, sultanas (golden raisins) or mixed dried fruit (fruit cake mix) to the dry mixture.

Shortbread

Do not be tempted to use margarine instead of butter – the flavour is never as good.

MAKES TWO 20 CM/8 IN ROUNDS

	METRIC	IMPERIAL	AMERICAN
Plain (all-purpose) flour	225 g	8 oz	2 cups
Cornflour (cornstarch)	100 g	4 oz	1 cup
A pinch of salt			
Caster (superfine) sugar, plus extra for sprinkling	100 g	4 oz	½ cup
Butter, diced	225 g	8 oz	1 cup

1 Mix the flours, salt and sugar, then, using your fingertips, rub in the butter until the mixture resembles breadcrumbs.

2 Press into two greased 20 cm/8 in sandwich tins (pans), prick all over with a fork and mark each one into eight segments. Chill for 1 hour.

3 Bake in a preheated oven at 150°C/300°F/gas mark 2 for 1 hour until lightly golden. Sprinkle with a little more caster sugar.

4 Leave to cool in the tins, then break into segments to serve.

⏱ **Preparation and cooking time:** 1¼ hours plus chilling

Index

TX 717.5 .K38 2001

Kavenagh, Carmel.

Traditional Irish cookery